Newcastle
CITY COUNCIL

Newcastle Libraries and Information Service

 **0191 277 4100**

Please return this item to any of Newcastle's Libraries by the last date shown above. If not requested by another customer the loan can be renewed, you can do this by phone, post or in person.

Charges may be made for late returns.

OLLY MURS
ON THE ROAD

CORONET

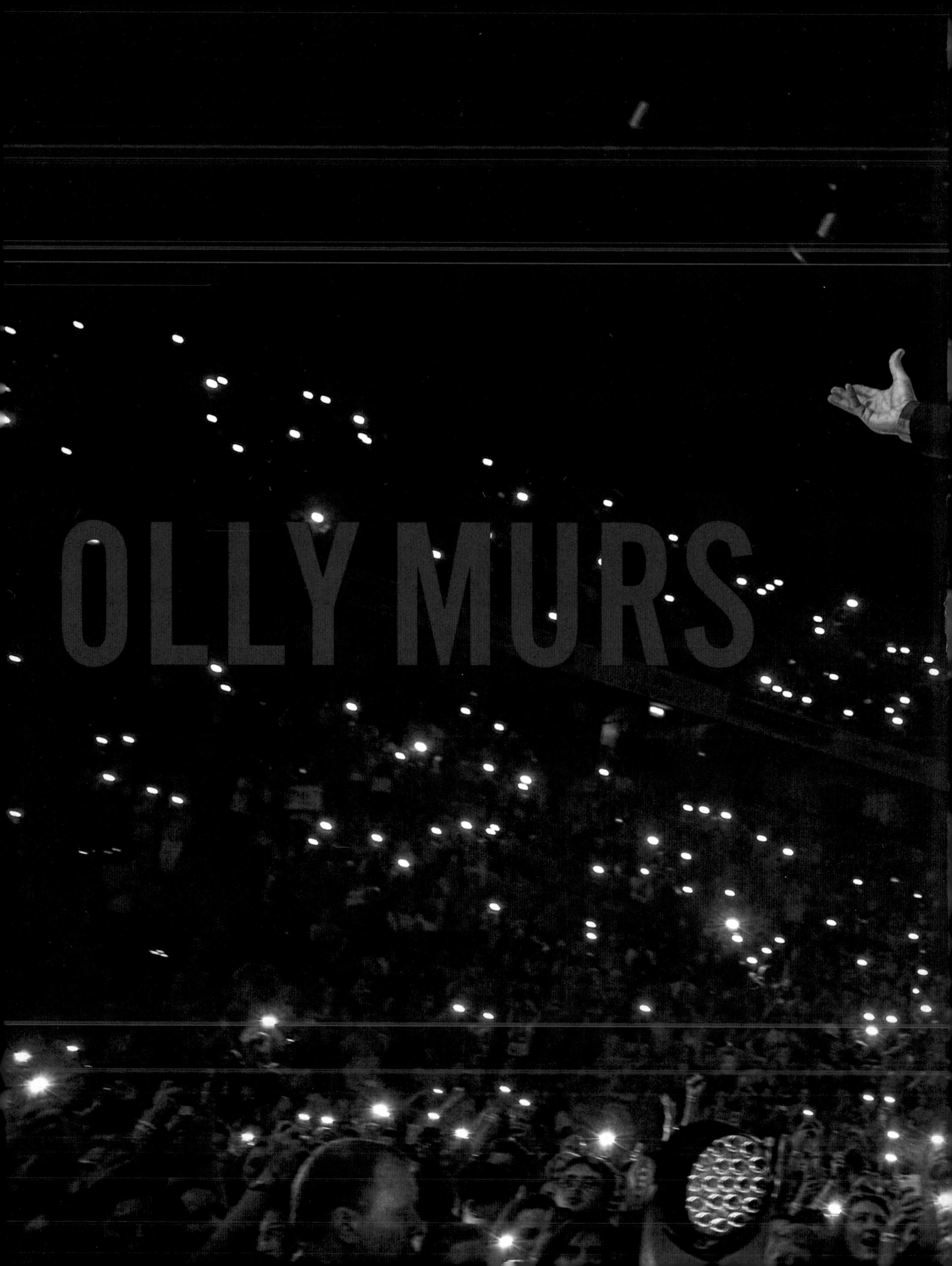
OLLY MURS

ON THE ROAD

WORDS BY MATT ALLEN

SOUNDCHECK

Jumping onstage in front of a crowd of 15,000 people will always be a funny business.

When the spotlight hits me, there's a huge noise; a wave of screams and cheering. I can see cameras flashing, and rows and rows of people filming me with their mobile phones. Wherever I look, everybody's eyes are focused upon me, waiting for my next move. And guess what? There's no better feeling. I live for performing in front of big crowds, playing my songs to the fans and dancing across the stage. All day, whenever I'm on tour, I'm just waiting for that moment. It's like a drug.

That might sound funny, but it's true. Think about it: I'm out front – it's just me, my name, my time in the limelight, and it's so intoxicating; a buzz that takes over my whole body, like the rush a footballer experiences if they score the winning goal in a cup final, or when an athlete stands on the podium with their Olympic gold medal. For me, that same sensation arrives when I'm up there singing in an arena, my name in lights behind me.

It first happened during my time on *X Factor*, when I was playing in front of studio audiences. In those days, my performances were being beamed in to the living rooms of millions of people across the country. Since then, I've stepped out of the shadows of the show, as a singer at least, and that feeling has got bigger and better with every year – first on my theatre tour in 2010, and later in arenas around the UK where I've played to audiences of 15,000 people. I have even supported the likes of Robbie Williams and One Direction, and sung to crowds of 70,000 people in massive stadiums. That was pretty special.

By the time I came to releasing my fourth record, *Never Been Better*, in 2014, I wanted to make the best live show possible. I had a whole set of singles and crowd favourites to choose from. There was also an army of fans that I wanted to entertain – *the best in the world* – so I was up for taking a show across the country that could give everybody a good time. And what a roller-coaster it was.

I played 28 dates, starting in Sheffield and ending in Liverpool. We travelled to Cardiff, Belfast, Dublin, Glasgow, Newcastle, Leeds, Manchester, Birmingham, Nottingham and London. Backed by my amazing 11-piece band, we had a great time on a stage that lit up like a spaceship from *Star Wars*. When I stepped on to it for the first time, it blew my mind – it looked amazing.

Then there was the love from my amazing fans. There were sell-out shows pretty much every night and those guys were dancing in their seats from the minute I arrived onstage, though some of the girls got a bit carried away. One or two of them even started throwing their underwear around – *cheeky*. But thanks to them, there was a party in every city I played. I had the time of my life.

There was a lot of craziness going on behind the scenes too, the stuff that my fans – you guys reading this book – rarely get to witness, or hear about. Some people think that I just rock up to the mic and start performing on a tour like *Never Been Better*, but the hard work actually began in Christmas 2014, when we first planned the performance. Later there were rehearsals, TV appearances and single releases. I had to pose with my Madame Tussauds waxwork model in Blackpool. I performed a surprise duet with Robbie Williams, and experienced a pranking at the hands of comedian John Bishop – onstage.

In Scotland, I even wore a kilt. In the middle of all that, I landed a job of co-presenter on *X Factor*, which was an amazing moment for me. By the end of it, I was bloody exhausted.

Not all of it was fun, either. There were a few backstage arguments and tabloid dramas along the way, not to mention a schedule of painful training sessions with my personal coach as I tried to get in shape for the road (wow, it hurt). I embarrassed myself on *This Morning* with Phillip Schofield and Amanda Holden (you'll read about that in chapter two), and I had to relive a shocking moment in Sheffield when I once ripped my trousers onstage. At times, the action seemed to be non-stop.

But a funny thing happened at the beginning of the year while I was in the rehearsal studios with my band: I realised that a lot of pop tours are a closed shop to the outside world, a proper mystery. I thought, *How many of my favourite artists have spoken about what life's really like on the road? And in juicy detail?* I couldn't think of many, and as we got closer to the opening night of the tour, I became determined to give my fans a glimpse into what the pop business can be like. So, for two months, author Matt Allen and photographer Christie Goodwin joined me on the bus. Their aim: to document the *Never Been Better* tour and deliver a no-holds-barred look at my biggest headline shows so far. Thanks to their words and photographs, you can now grab your very own Access All Areas pass and join me backstage, in these pages.

I hope you enjoy the ride.

#NEVERBEENBETTERTOUR

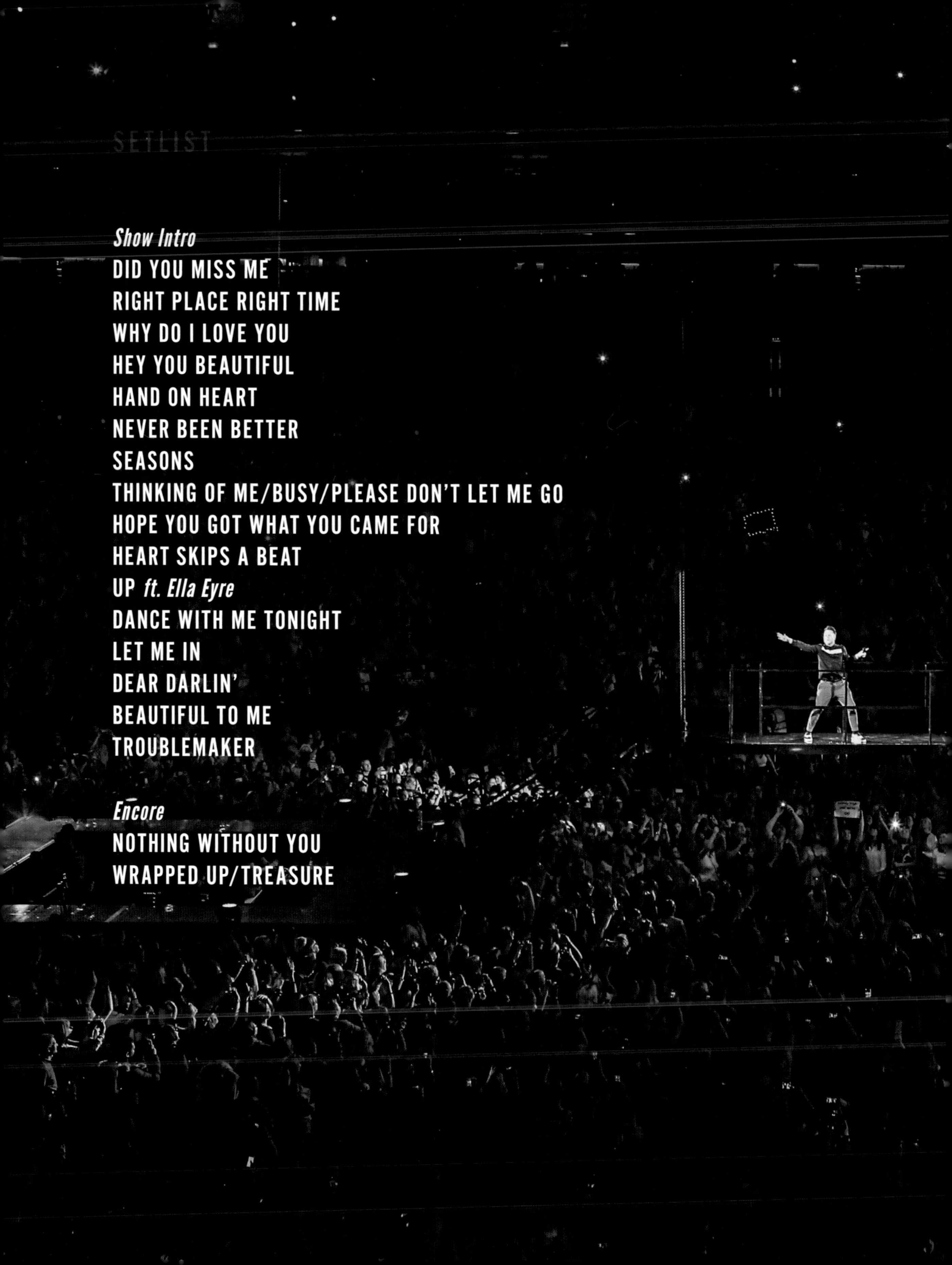

Show Intro

DID YOU MISS ME

RIGHT PLACE RIGHT TIME

WHY DO I LOVE YOU

HEY YOU BEAUTIFUL

HAND ON HEART

NEVER BEEN BETTER

SEASONS

THINKING OF ME/BUSY/PLEASE DON'T LET ME GO

HOPE YOU GOT WHAT YOU CAME FOR

HEART SKIPS A BEAT

UP *ft. Ella Eyre*

DANCE WITH ME TONIGHT

LET ME IN

DEAR DARLIN'

BEAUTIFUL TO ME

TROUBLEMAKER

Encore

NOTHING WITHOUT YOU

WRAPPED UP/TREASURE

TOUR DATES

MARCH
31st Sheffield, Motorpoint Arena

APRIL
1st Sheffield, Motorpoint Arena
3rd Cardiff, Motorpoint Arena
4th Cardiff, Motorpoint Arena

7th Belfast, Odyssey Arena
8th Belfast, Odyssey Arena

10th Dublin, 3Arena
11th Dublin, 3Arena
12th Dublin, 3Arena

14th Glasgow, The SSE Hydro
15th Glasgow, The SSE Hydro
16th Glasgow, The SSE Hydro

18th Newcastle, Metro Radio Arena
19th Newcastle, Metro Radio Arena

20th Leeds, First Direct Arena

22nd Manchester, Manchester Arena
23rd Manchester, Manchester Arena
24th Manchester, Manchester Arena

26th Birmingham, Barclaycard Arena
27th Birmingham, Barclaycard Arena
28th Birmingham, Barclaycard Arena

30th Nottingham, Capital FM Arena

MAY
1st Nottingham, Capital FM Arena

3rd London, The O2
4th London, The O2
5th London, The O2
7th London, The O2

9th Liverpool, Echo Arena

THE VOICE

Olly Murs is warming up his vocal chords in a southwest London rehearsal studio. He 'ummms', he 'aahhhhs'; his pursed lips vibrate as he makes a series of strangely-muted 'wet raspberry' noises. Close your eyes and it's hard not to picture a kid gunning the engines of his imaginary racing car. Then the performance takes a surreal twist. Olly pulls what looks like a plastic party straw from his Manchester United kitbag and blows into it hard.

Pfffffffftttttzzzzzzzz! Pfffffffftttttzzzzzzzz!

With a swift gulp of air he breathes into the straw again. His cheeks swell up like an expanding puffer fish.

Pfffffffftttttzzzzzzzz! Pfffffffftttttzzzzzzzz! Pfffffffftttttzzzzzzzz!

There's more…

Pfffffffftttttzzzzzzzz! Pfffffffftttttzzzzzzzz! Pfffffffftttttzzzzzzzz!

This time though, a hooky melody emerges from the buzz. It's the intro to 'Never Been Better', title track to Olly's 2014 number one album and an infectiously upbeat 'middle finger' to the people that once doubted his unstoppable charge from *X Factor* runner-up in 2009, to his current standing as one of Britain's Biggest Pop Stars.

'*Burning from the sky, there's no gravity. Hunger in my eyes, nothing stopping me.*'

These defiant lyrics arrived seemingly radio-primed last year, but there's nothing in the way of his instantly memorable, me-against-the-world bravado now. Olly's too busy parping away on that plastic straw.

Pfffffffftttttzzzzzzzz! Pfffffffftttttzzzzzzzz! Pfffffffftttttzzzzzzzz!

'I look like a right idiot,' he says, suddenly relaxing. 'I was taught this technique by a throat therapist. It stretches my voice and stops me from over-singing, or damaging my vocal chords.'

And it works?

'Well, apparently they tested it on the Aerosmith singer, Steven Tyler. A load of Harley Street doctors went in to see him with the straw. Afterwards, he reckoned it was the best he'd sung in years.'

Olly takes a settling breath.

'Let's do some more warm-ups,' says Kevin Leo, vocal coach and the singer's one-man harmony support unit. For the past few minutes he's been watching studiously as Olly runs through his scales in descending order. Kev (everyone calls him 'Kev') folds his arms, his shoulders pressed to the wall like a mechanic assessing a revving engine. Only a rolled-up newspaper and cuppa remains absent from his profile.

'Ascending this time, Oll...'

'*Aaaaahhhhhhhh...*'

Kev's worked wonders since first being hired to coach with Olly in 2009. Back then, before the hit records and sold out tours, Olly had finished with *X Factor*, the TV show created by music impresario, Simon Cowell and launch pad to Olly's now impressive chart career (three number one albums and counting; four number one singles in the bag, plus a portfolio of sold-out arena shows). Despite the hype surrounding his emergence, fine-tuning was needed, especially if Olly was to make a serious charge at top-billing status.

Anyone looking over his CV would have spotted the glitches; the 'Previous Experience' section made for patchy reading. Prior to an impressive *X Factor* debut – his cover of Stevie Wonder's 'Superstition' wooed judges during the televised auditions – Olly had started on a karaoke machine in his local pub in Essex. This was followed by short spells fronting local pub bands, the Small Town Blaggers and F2K. Meanwhile, his closest brush with stardom arrived during an appearance on *Deal or No Deal* when he walked away with a tenner. Despite finishing second to Joe McElderry on *X Factor*, Olly was a little rough around the edges, and everyone knew it.

'I was a singer that hadn't sung a lot,' he says, now chewing on his straw. 'Pros sing from the age of ten. I didn't start until I was 23. Having said that, I'm one of the longest-serving *X Factor* finalists now. I'm still going. Everyone has fallen away. JLS aren't around anymore. One Direction started after me...' He raises his arms, triumphantly. 'Olly Murs! Still surviving!'

He's joking, but only a little.

This longevity wasn't assured at the beginning, however. When Olly initially struggled to nail the recording of breakout single 'Please Don't Let Me Go', Kev was hired. A piano-led singing session in his Fulham workspace kick-started a chart-topping recording splurge, their labour culminating in Olly's self-titled album that same year – the fastest selling debut of 2010. Five years on, Kev's now a regular part of the backroom staff, where his drills and routines strengthen Olly's vocal chords before any gruelling singing shifts, such as a lengthy tour or recording session.

Kev nods towards Olly. 'He works hard,' he says proudly, though he reckons his client is prone to the odd crisis of self-belief, maybe more so than other artists.

'Yeah, I used to think I was a crap singer, a shit singer, didn't I, Kev?' says Olly. 'Sometimes I'll lose a bit of confidence and say, "I'm not very good am I?"

And he'll go, "Stop saying that. You're not crap, it's just that we have to make you stronger, to get your voice out." He told me to stop worrying about other singers, to do my own thing.'

Olly seems restless today, like he has a point to prove.

'I'd love to have more power,' says Olly.

Kev nods. 'Yeah, but you don't have to be *perfect*,' he says soothingly, like a teacher talking down a fidgety pupil. 'With opera singers, I use keyboards so they can hit their notes exactly. Not with you. A pop singer's different to an opera singer – they have to sing pure notes. I want you to sound raw. I want you to sound like Olly Murs.'

That rawness is there today for sure, but not all of it is welcome. Olly runs a finger around his gums, pulling a face. He hasn't cleaned his teeth this morning. His throat's beginning to tickle.

'I'm dry,' he says. 'I didn't mouthwash, either. I can feel the bacteria and it's so annoying. I've been singing for the last three days and I have to sing for two hours again now. It's like I'm training for a marathon.'

Kev nods sympathetically. 'OK, Oll. *Ascending*.'

'*Aaaaahhhhhhhh...*'

—

Kev's appearance feels important today. He only buzzes into Olly's orbit whenever there's work to be done, and SW19 studios currently has an expectant energy zinging between its walls. It might not look much from the outside, what with its position in the heart of a Wimbledon industrial estate, set back from an avenue of building yards and parked lorries. But it's from this modest space that preparations for one of the biggest pop events of 2015 are being finalised: the rehearsals for Olly's *Never Been Better* tour, a sold-out, 28-date UK extravaganza that includes four nights at London's cavernous 02 Arena, three nights in Dublin, Manchester, Birmingham and Glasgow.

Inside SW19, a large studio space has been given over to Olly and his touring musicians. Stacks of flight cases line the room. A mixing desk stands in one corner.

Olly's 11-strong band are positioned in a tight circle as everyone preps for a long day of rehearsals. Bassist Ben Lyonsmyth and guitarist Rupert Fenn fire out a seam of barraging funk riffs, drummer Dexter Hercules tunes his kit; the brass section, Kenji Fenton (sax), Mike Davis (trumpet) and Paul Burton (trombone), run through scales and check the setlist on their iPads.

It's here, under the keen ears of keyboardist and musical director Sean Barry, that Olly's bombastic live sound is currently being fine-tuned. The culmination of an intense planning process, the show's arrangements and programming sessions first began with Olly and Sean after Christmas 2014, with full band rehearsals beginning in February. Now, following a two-week promotional trip to America and Japan, this latest round of sessions are set to finesse the show. The mood is buzzy, but there's an empty space in the middle of the room where a microphone stand has been placed. Work's due to start, but there's no sign of The Voice clocking in just yet.

'He's not that keen on getting started, obviously,' says one of the techs walking through the studio, cocking his head towards the window. 'He's still down there, watching videos.'

He's right. A quick glance into the car park below confirms that, yes, Olly's now in his motor, sitting alongside tour manager and 'best mate', Mark Murphy. Everyone's spotted the pair scrolling through their phones, laughing. Good news: there's no rush on today.

—

Back in 2003, Olly went to his first ever gig. He was 18, nearly 19. Justin Timberlake's Justified World Tour had arrived at the London Docklands Arena and Olly – a fan – bought tickets with a college mate, Jamie. His parents often went to shows, the likes of The Jam and The Specials, and Olly quite fancied the same Big Experience. When it finally arrived, an exciting realisation dawned on him: he'd never seen so many women in one place.

'That sounds ridiculous, I know,' he laughs. 'But when you're at school, or college, you're with girls. But I'd never been in a room, a venue, with so many.'

Then his focus changed.

'I was in awe of what Timberlake was doing,' he says. 'It was weird. I didn't think I was going to be a pop star at that stage, but something inside me was saying it was something I was supposed to do. I analysed his every move afterwards. His chat. His every spoken moment. I was mesmerised by him.'

And 12 years on, you're here.

'Yeah. It took me five years to pluck up the courage to give it a go, though. I'm glad I did. It's crazy to think that I now do what he was doing then...'

—

Back in the studio, Olly finally checks in for work, dressed in grey trackie bottoms, black cardigan, brown suede loafers and white tee. His chin is peppered with a day's worth of stubble. The mood sharpens. He's a bundle of raw energy; adrenalised, bounding from person to person like an overexcited puppy; that cheeky grin is cut across his chops. He updates everyone on his newly-styled, swept up quiff ('Makes me look younger, don't it?') and his morning training session with Mark ('He was only sick in a bin!'). He jokes with his backing vocalists, Darren Ellison, John Allen, Katie Holmes and Louise Bagan, the foursome kicking back on studio stools.

'Feeling nicely rested, girls?' he asks, all mock concern. 'Good, because those chairs are going tomorrow and you're gonna be knackered.'

He paces the circle of musicians.

'I want to see happiness!' he shouts.

He leans over the sound screen that separates the band from Dexter's deafening drum grooves and slaps a cymbal.

'I'm buzzing to lose my voice!'

There's an outbreak of The Pointer Sisters. 'I'm so excited and I just can't hide it,' he croons, laughing. He's hyping himself up, locating the right mood for an intense day at the office.

'Let's blitz it,' he tells Sean. 'I wanna sing the lot. I just want to do the set as it is. Let's see if we can get it in the bag.'

As with everything Olly has achieved so far – his career ascent from music TV charmer and arena-packing pop star, to effervescent telly host – rehearsal sessions run at one speed only, full tilt, the band opening with 'Misirlou' by Dick Dale & His Del-Tones, the spiky guitar instrumental made famous by Quentin Tarantino's movie *Pulp Fiction*. When the brass section brings a jazzy swing to Rupert's machine-gunning guitar notes, Olly holds firm in the middle of the room, hands in pockets, arms spread wide. He's stretching the fabric of his cardigan like Batman blowing out a cape.

A run of fan favourites is ushered in with 'Did You Miss Me', a powerful introduction to Olly's sashaying vocal range. Kev's session has warmed his singing pipes considerably. That straw seems to have helped, too.

'Bruce Springsteen's probably one of the greatest singers around,' Olly says. 'He gets out there, smokes a cigarette and just sings. Each to their own. But I feel like I'm an Olympic athlete, like Usain Bolt. Would he run 100 metres without stretching for an hour? No way. I have to do the same, but with my voice.'

This is the first in a short series of low-key rehearsals. At the end of the week, work begins on a fully operational stage in Wakefield. Very little is being held in reserve, though. Olly grooves with the same levels of excitement as a performer playing to a packed stadium, prowling in front of his musicians and shuffling his feet to the rhythm. His gestures range from fist pumps to pleading hand grabs as 'Right Place Right Time', 'Why Do I Love You' and 'Hey You Beautiful' zip by. Before 'Stick With Me', he thanks an imaginary Manchester crowd for their applause. There are urges for the O2 to hurry to their seats during the intro to 'Never Been Better'. 'London, you best be back from your toilet break!' he shouts from his second floor studio in a Wimbledon industrial estate.

'This show is pumped from the get go,' he says later. 'As soon as the intro starts, and then "Did You Miss Me" kicks in, you'll wanna go out and get smashed. You'll want to go to the merch stand, buy an Olly Murs shot glass and party.'

You're selling Olly Murs shot glasses?

'Er, no, actually. Maybe we should, though...'

Some of his more offbeat flashes today won't make the final cut. 'Heart Skips A Beat' loses a little momentum as Olly checks his phone for messages. He then reveals a flash of belly to Kenji, Mike and Paul, before dropping to the floor for a series of GI Jane-style, one-armed push-ups (he manages three). Later, heart-bruised ballad 'Dear Darlin'' is delivered lying down, knees pointing skywards.

With over an hour of performance gone, his energy levels are drooping. There are calls for something more upbeat. Sean suggests a planned live medley that pulses together Chic's 'Le Freak', 'Working Day And Night' by Michael Jackson, plus the souped-up chorus to Mark Ronson's 2014 hit 'Uptown Funk', in what's set to be a rousing highpoint within the show's finale.

'Yeah, let's do this!!' shouts Olly. 'I want to wake up. I want to dance.'

At times, just watching him is exhausting.

'Yeah, and I'm only running at 70%,' he says. 'This is nothing.'

Sarah Gallagher, his manager at Modest!, has arrived to make comments on the setlist. She first started working with Olly during the final stages of his so-nearly triumphant *X Factor* season, and has managed his day-to-day celebrity ever since. Notes are being taken on his delivery, the sharpness of his live tracks. 'He loves rehearsing,' she says. 'He loves performing. He's in his element... Basically, Olly loves showing off.'

He turns to face his imaginary audience, somewhere in Liverpool, Sheffield, or Newcastle, his arms outstretched again.

'Come on guys, sing with me!' he shouts. 'Scream! *Scream!*'

—

Currently, Olly is 30, or '29 plus one'. Plus two isn't far away from the tour's close. Despite being in the music industry for over six years, he's never taken drugs in his life. He says he doesn't need to. But performing live is the closest he'll ever get to feeling wasted.

'What I hear from other artists is that being onstage, in front of the big crowd, is like the high,' he says. 'It's addictive. Nothing compares to walking out in front of 20,000 people and hearing that cheer, and feeling the excitement, that buzz.'

The first time he experienced this rush arrived with *X Factor* in 2009. After a week of 'boot camp' rehearsals with his mentor, Simon Cowell, Olly settled on singing the Elton John single 'Your Song'. He was to perform in front of a live audience at London's Hammersmith Apollo, where the programme was recorded. He knew it was a safe choice for his vocal range – Simon did, too. Then his performance was a bit duff. 'I didn't do that great, I didn't sing well,' he admits.

The crowd reaction gave him everything he needed, though. Affirmation and adulation. A little love.

'I was feeding off them,' he says. 'They were shouting, they were screaming, they were whistling at me. I thought, *Wow this is pretty awesome!* I just naturally felt a connection with me being onstage, doing it as a job, and them being fans. I was like, *I can do this full time!*'

He's relaxed now. His two hours of strenuous rehearsals are complete, it's been a productive day. With just over a week until the first night in Sheffield – 'D-Day approaching,' as he describes it – Olly's hitting his marks for showtime – 'I'm making sure I'm prepared, so I can give the fans the best possible show.'

There's always pressure on the eve of a big tour like this one, he says, but shutting out the stress is relatively easy. Besides, his aim isn't to win over the army of hardcore fans – they're already in the bag and he knows they'll love the songs. It's the doubters he's keen to convince. The reluctant boyfriends in tow; the dads and friends of real fans along for a night out – 'I want to prove them wrong.'

Of all the things he's done with his life so far – college, his previous job in an Essex call centre, playing football – performing live is the role that has given Olly the most confidence. 'No matter who's in front of me, the press, the industry that are against me sometimes, if anyone comes to my show, I want them to walk away smiling, regardless. They've got to leave their ego at the door, though. They need to come in and have a good time and enjoy what I do. Don't be worrying about where I came from. Have an open mind. It can be exhausting getting it right, but that's our job, isn't it?'

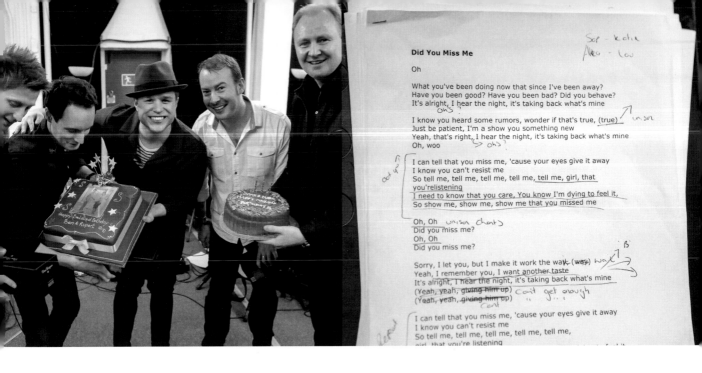

So you see this as a job, then?

He shrugs his shoulders. 'I dunno. I don't find touring a job. I find a lot of the other things a job. Like if I'm doing press interviews, red carpet events or stuff like that. I wouldn't miss doing photoshoots. I'd go as far to say that even though there's an excitement when I know I've written a great song in the studio, I wouldn't miss that too much, either. But I come alive onstage. If I've had an argument with my girlfriend, or if I'm in a bad mood, or something's happened to put me in a bad place... as soon as the first song kicks in, I forget about everything.'

He seems to be replaying that freedom in his head, hearing the noise of his *Pulp Fiction*-inspired intro and seeing his crowd stretched out in front of him.

'This show's in your face,' he says. 'They're gonna go bonkers. The fans are going to kick off, mate.'

OLLY ON THE RECORD: THE SHOWMAN

Being a showman is in my DNA. I've always done it, but I probably only realised it was in me when I started going clubbing with my mates in Essex. That's when I got it into my head that I could dance. I would break out moves in front of my mates and try to pull the ladies; I liked to have a bit of a giggle – that was my role in the group. No one else could dance like me and I was always joking around. I loved being the centre of attention.

But I've always had that streak in me: it comes from the Murs family genes, and we've always got on the mic at karaoke nights. Recently we discovered that Dad's side of the family were circus performers, like my great-great-gran. On my mum's side, my Auntie Pat was a singer, as was my great-nan. She would never say she was a professional, but she used to sing in clubs, performing old Cockney songs.

We've always been a very confident family, on Mum's side especially, where the idea of entertaining and making people feel good has always been there. You could never say we were a shy family. We've always been a very fun, happy lot, so if you ever come into our house you'll have to be willing to get on the mic and sing a song, dance till your socks come off, and have a bloody good time. That attitude has been so infectious throughout my life.

Like when I started clubbing. I'd always wind my mates up about it, I'd say, 'Lads, none of you can dance like me.' I was a good mover. I used to watch a lot of MTV videos and there were always so many amazing dancers and dance routines. I liked to copy the moves. I had good rhythm. All the girls would come around us when I was having a laugh on the dance floor. Yeah, I used to do alright back then, but it's amazing what a makeover, some newspaper attention and *X Factor* can do for you.

So, because of my family, the singing and the dancing merged into me, but I don't know if I'm driven to be an entertainer. I guess I'll only discover that if it gets taken away from me, but I can't predict how I'll react if that happens. I always say this to my girlfriend and my family: I really don't know how it's gonna affect me when my career ends. It could be terrible. It could mean that I go a bit crazy. I might miss it so badly that I don't know where to go or what to do. I might get depressed. I might be sad. Though I'd like to think I'll be fine. But you see a lot of artists who struggle. They come away from this industry and they miss it so much that it causes problems in their personal lives.

For now I'm just living in the moment. Being a showman is a roller-coaster ride. I'm in it, and I'm loving it.

Chapter Two

'OLLY'S HEAD ON THE TABLE, PLEASE...'

'OLLY'S HEAD ON THE TABLE, PLEASE...'

When Olly arrives at London's ITV Studios alongside Mark for a day's filming two days later, he looks tired. It's been a gruelling 48 hours, full of training and rehearsals. He also went to his nan's funeral yesterday.

But there is no rest in view, Sarah has a hectic itinerary mapped out for today. It starts at lunchtime chat show, *Loose Women*, and ends with an appearance on *The Jonathan Ross Show* later this evening. Afterwards, the team will make a long drive to Wakefield for a weekend of production rehearsals before Olly's opening night.

'I haven't slept well,' he says, settling into his dressing room. 'It's been crazy.'

He looks up at the TV. Hollywood actor Russell Crowe is a guest on daytime national treasure, *This Morning*. He's chatting to presenters, Phillip Schofield and Amanda Holden. Olly's eyes light up.

'Hang on, that's only down the corridor, isn't it?' He grabs his phone. 'Come on, Mark,' he says. 'I'm getting a selfie.'

They wander around ITV's backstage avenues, seeking out the studio. When Olly arrives, there's no gladiatorial superstar in sight. The interview, it turns out, was recorded a week previously, but a production team member suggests he could still 'pop in' to say hello to Pip, Amanda and the audience at home. They can all make fun of the fact he'd mistakenly thought the interview was being filmed live. That's if he fancies it?

Mark calls and checks in with Sarah. Is temporarily hijacking *This Morning* a good idea? She's not so sure, what with their other commitments to ITV. There might be an exclusivity issue to deal with. But it's too late. Olly's face is already on the screen, grinning broadly, sandwiched between Schofield and Holden. Sarah, still in the dressing room, watches the scene unfolding live on telly, shaking her head. She's half-smiling, half-bemused at his latest escapade.

Olly's been in the building for less than five minutes.

—

Olly's fame is intrinsically linked with the telly. When he first burst onto the pop platform in a pork pie hat and too tight trousers, it was as the wiggling, baby-faced Essex-boy-turned-pop-voice. He had the cheek, plenty of jokes. Girls loved his chat, lads could appreciate his geezerish, down-the-pub persona. Mums and grannies wanted to mollycoddle him. Olly had arrived seemingly ready-made for TV, later hosting *Xtra Factor* with Caroline Flack. His own Saturday prime time show, *A Night In With Olly Murs*, followed in 2014.

Such is his ever-expanding national superstardom that Madame Tussauds have commissioned a waxwork of Olly's likeness for their Blackpool museum. The model, six months in the making, is here, brought to ITV for the finishing touches on hair and skin tones. It stands in a dressing room, life-sized, leaning forwards in an onstage position, clobber provided by Olly's management team – grey trousers, white shirt, black tasselled shoes. A microphone, stand and burgundy braces complete the look. As does that famous, cheeky chappy grin.

Olly stumbles into his likeness and does a double take. He freezes, his jaw drooping. Mark, Sarah and long-term hair stylist Mellissa Brown laugh as they catch his reaction, the sensation of being greeted with a near perfect clone has weirded Olly out.

'Bloody hell, that... is... *freaky*!' he says. As always, a little innuendo is never too far away: 'Can I touch myself?'

He closes in on the statue, teasing its hair and caressing the stubble. 'Holy shit, that's terrifying.'

Then he glances down at the waistline. There's a slight wince. 'Oh my god, I look like a right fat bastard!'

Mark cuts in. 'You were a fat bastard.'

Olly introduces himself to the Madame Tussauds crew, in attendance to add the finishing flourishes to his likeness. A make-up artist discusses styling products with Mellissa – the type of self-tanning lotions he prefers, hair wax. No detail is considered too small if they're to get his replica 100% accurate.

'Will you be tanning for the tour, Olly?' someone asks.

'Oh yeah, I've got a few sunbed sessions booked in over the weekend,' he says. 'Those big screens onstage are gonna be HD so I've gotta look half decent!' Notes are made. They will darken the model in the coming days to match his onstage tones.

He takes selfies with the figure as a make-up artist mixes a palette of skin shades alongside his face. It's time to apply the correct colour around the eyes, though the process sounds excruciating. 'Let's put Olly's head on the table, please,' suggests one of the creative team, Sarah wincing as the model's cranium is neatly decapitated with a swift crack of the neck. Olly gazes into the synthetic blue eyes as his bust passes across the room.

'Go on, you've always wanted to kiss yourself,' says Mark, leaning into his ear. 'Now's the chance.'

—

Olly and Mark are having an argument. It's something that seems to happen on a daily basis, though the bickering's mostly light-hearted. Battleground topics often involve football (Olly supports Manchester United; Mark's a fan of their hated rivals, Liverpool), or a recent sporting competition between the two – pool, a game of tennis, a PlayStation session, maybe. As they relax in the green room, Mark is laughing at Olly's claim that, given the chance, he'd have worked out between telly commitments today. Apparently, his mate, TV presenter Jeff Brazier, mentioned a nearby gym when they bumped into each other earlier.

'You wouldn't have,' laughs Mark.

Olly tries to warn him off. 'Don't...'

He repeats the challenge. 'You wouldn't have.'

'I would,' says Olly, frowning.

'You wouldn't have,' Mark says.

'How can you say that, Mark?' snaps Olly, clearly annoyed.

'Because I've known you over five years,' says Mark.

The pair first met in 2009, during the recording of *X Factor*. Olly was yet to reach the final, but Mark, who had already worked with Modest!, had been impressed by his stage presence. 'I thought he was a star from day one. I saw him perform and knew he was a pop sensation. I told him, "I want to tour manage you when this is finished,"' he says.

Olly was confused. 'What the hell's a tour manager?'

By the time of the final, Mark had been granted his wish. Olly signed with Modest! and was placed under his care for future touring commitments. It was Mark's job to run every aspect of the live schedule. Olly's career path was still uncertain at that point, but Mark told him he'd get a record deal, that he'd tour the UK and sell albums around the world. 'Olly, you'll even win awards if you get your head down and work hard for the next six months,' he said.

Olly thought he was mad. 'Mark had so much faith in me,' he says. 'I believed in myself, but I didn't really think it was gonna get to where it is now. He just believed in what he saw and what he felt was gonna happen. He was very confident. We've been friends ever since.'

He says the pair have had their moments. They can battle over work issues, especially when they've been in each other's pocket for too long on tour. 'Mark's been my best mate for a long time now, we naturally spend a lot of time together,' he says. 'You can't fake a friendship. But as soon as we go to work, we go into that mode. He'll ask me questions. I'll battle with him. We've had our arguments through the years, as everyone does, as every mate does, but we forgive and forget. Then we move on.'

Their latest matey duel hinges on fitness. Together, the pair are working with Olly's personal trainer, Rob Solly. Their aim: to get trim for the UK tour. Olly has even taken to juicing and a portion-control diet to shift weight. Today's pre-cooked dinner comprises lemon and sesame seed-crusted chicken with winter coleslaw. His exercise in self-restraint has shaved eight pounds from his frame already.

'It's important to look good onstage,' he explains. 'I don't want to have a belly. This last year and a half, I've been a lazy bastard.'

The turning point arrived in January. 'I kept saying, "I feel fat." I'd look at myself and think, "What's happened? Why do I feel so lazy?"'

At first Olly thought it might be something to do with being in a long-term relationship with Francesca, his girlfriend of three years, who he met at a house party in Essex. 'I'm thinking, "Is that the reason? Because we sit in a lot and watch TV..." That's probably a part of it. I always joke around with her. I'll say, "I'm eating all this food because of you." And she'll say, "Well I'm getting fat because of *you*..." I blame everyone.'

Currently, he's training four times a week, though the physical exertion of touring will keep him trim, he reckons. For now, there are morning sessions with Rob, where he works out alongside Mark. The boxing drills are 'brutal'. Olly reckons the pair aren't that competitive, though.

Mark snorts. 'What are you talking about, Oll?'

Olly ignores the dig and places another party straw between his lips. *Pffffffftttttzzzzzzzz!*

—

Despite the headlining gigs, TV appearances and celebrity showboating, Olly reckons he's a little bit shy sometimes. There are occasions when he's uncomfortable as the centre of attention; 'The Big I Am' is a card he's reluctant to play.

'I don't like making a fuss when I walk into the room,' he says. 'I don't like to walk in to *anywhere* and cause a drama.'

Sure, he enjoys the flashes of recognition. The autograph hunters, the girls that approach him on the street to say hello – that's always nice, if they're not overly aggressive or super-pushy. The requests for Instagram pictures are a manageable fallout from his celebrity, too. But away from the stage, Olly would much rather be anonymous. 'A shadow,' as he calls it.

'Mark, Sarah, my mates will tell you, I don't like to walk into a bar, restaurant or nightclub, or here even, and be the loudest guy in the room,' he says. 'That might surprise people. They watch me perform, they see how confident I am onstage and they think I'm like that all the time. But I'm sometimes quite shy when I'm with people. I don't like to be in their face. Even when someone comes up to me and says, "Hi, my name's Steve." I never go, "Hello mate," like they know who I am. I say, "Hi Steve, I'm Olly. Nice to meet you."'

He hates the thought of being a diva. Even the rider, the food prepared for him backstage, can be 'just the basics,' he says. 'I've seen artists treat a rider like it's their shopping list. They tell a venue what they want, it turns up, and they'll take it home to their fridge. I can't be doing that.'

As Madame Tussauds apply the finishing touches to his face, a producer from the *Loose Women* team runs through the issues they'd like Olly to discuss on air. She scans her clipboard, carefully suggesting the more delicate topics. There's a section on childbirth selfies, 'all the rage', apparently. She then mentions Zayn Malik, the One Direction singer, also managed by Modest!. His recent split from the boy band has every tabloid brimming with headlines and rumour. Sarah is worried Olly might be swamped with questions and doesn't want any controversial enquiries. She also knows he can 'talk for England' on just about anything and a comment regarding One Direction is sure to make headlines.

For a second, he fantasises about an escape from the limelight. 'If I was Zayn, I'd be taking a six-month break,' he announces to the room. 'I'd have shaved my hair off, grown a beard and gone on holiday.'

He laughs. 'Who am I kidding? I can't take six months off. It couldn't happen... I hate being bored. Right, Sarah?'

The producer makes notes. She suggests that Olly not kiss all four members of the *Loose Women* panel when he makes his way into the studio. Apparently it eats up too much air time. He can't help himself, however. Moments later, he's planting a smacker on all four – Gloria Hunniford, Linda Robson, Nadia Sawalha

and Andrea McLean – before checking his phone's Twitter account. His mum, Vicky, has tweeted the show ('@Mrsfuzzymuzzy: Lunch Ready @loosewomen please be gentle with him ladies lol'). He plugs the tour and jokingly lies about his age again. ('I'm not 30, just yet,' he says, pulling a face. 'Twenty-nine plus one.') Before he goes, Olly grabs a *Loose Women* mug. 'For me mum,' he smiles.

'I told you he was cute,' coos Andrea. 'All the girls will be queuing up for you after the break...'

So much for not making a drama.

—

All this talk of tours has brought Olly back to his first ever live performance, a pub gig with the band Small Town Blaggers in his hometown of Witham, a unit he formed with local guitarist Jon Goodey in 2007. Olly was in a bad place back then. He'd left college with an NVQ in Sport and Recreation and had no real idea of what to do next. He'd just broken up with his girlfriend. Injury had cut short a semi-pro football career. His mood wasn't being helped by that disastrous *Deal or No Deal* appearance, either. That same year, Olly had turned down £26,000 in the game's bartering stages and walked away with next to nothing. The show had made him a temporary laughing stock in Witham – 'That hurt me badly,' he says. People even hassled him in his local pub, The George.

There was no real ambition to be a singer in that period. 'I think I had talent,' he says. 'But hardly any real self-belief.' Still, on a whim he threw himself into an *X Factor* audition, 'for a laugh'. Olly was 23, with nothing to lose, though his rendition of 'I Wanna Be Like You', the pop jangle from Disney's hit movie, *The Jungle Book* failed to impress the show's production crew. He was dismissed in the first round of try-outs.

But there's a defiant streak in him – 'I like to prove people wrong,' he says – and when his karaoke sessions in The George gathered a regular crowd, it was suggested he should start a band of his own. That's when he hooked up with Jon to learn a series of covers, acoustic tracks mostly, with some older pop hits thrown in, such as Erasure's 'A Little Respect' and The Killers' 'Mr Brightside.' Their first gig was a hit, he reports, looking chuffed.

'I performed the songs round my nan's house first of all,' he says. 'That was a bit weird, playing the family a load of covers. But the pub gig was on an Easter Sunday, so we got all the boys down there and everyone got involved, everyone was getting drunk. It wasn't rubbish. It was a good atmosphere. Then a fight broke out in the corner of the room. It got split up, but it kicked off again in the car park. Maybe our music turned people into louts.'

There were nerves then, but not the kind he experiences now. In 2007, the pressure was only small-time. Olly had low expectations, so did his crowd. All he

was hoping for was a good night out. 'Now people are spending money they've worked seriously hard for to see me play live,' he says. 'But I'll give my fans blood, sweat and tears on that stage and they'll know it. As long as I walk off feeling I've given it everything, there's nothing else I can do.'

—

Olly is about to cause a tabloid kerfuffle, and there's been a few of those over the years. With a new series of *X Factor* looming, he's been asked to present the show with friend and TV host, Caroline Flack, as the replacement for long-term frontman, Dermot O'Leary. With his decision to leave, the time is right for a Simon Cowell-inspired revamp, and Olly is very much at the forefront of his plans. A meeting has been scheduled during his day at ITV.

This feels a little bit strange for Olly. Dermot cajoled him through those nerve-wracking, live *X Factor* episodes in 2009. Two years later, they even trekked across the North Kenyan desert together for Comic Relief. 'He's the main man,' says Olly.

'Olly sees him as a good mate,' Sarah explains. She reckons a personal call to Dermot, or a lunch, will help to smooth things over.

'I don't want to step on anyone's toes,' says Olly. 'But I'm interested. I did *Xtra Factor* with Caroline for two years, it really helped my career. It helped me as a person. I got more confident in front of the camera, and onstage.'

That's not the only thing troubling him today, though. That Madame Tussauds waxwork: does it make him look, well, a little old? He's scanning his phone for the photos, zooming in on the model's face for evidence.

'God, it's weird,' he says. 'I'm annoyed that my eyes don't quite look right.'

Mellissa, now styling his hair for a performance of latest single 'Seasons' for *The Jonathan Ross Show*, leans over his shoulder. 'Your eyelids don't look like that,' she says. 'They look too baggy. I think you look old there.' The comments aren't helping.

Sarah has her say moments later. 'Remember you've lost eight pounds since then, babe,' she says, joking. 'Maybe you had fatter eyelids?'

He's dressed for show time now, with a black bomber jacket, tan tee and matching socks which are revealed by ankle-cropped black jeans. Mark can't help but playfully jab at the get-up. He points at Olly's high hems. 'Bloody hell, Oll, you expecting floods or what?'

Despite Mellissa's scissor work, he drops that once trademarked pork pie hat onto his head as he steps into the set's stage, which has been placed in front of a backdrop of dripping neon lights. This first performance is only a run through, so he keeps plenty in reserve, bouncing on the spot as he cruises through the lyrics at half strength.

'Listen honey, to every word I say, I know that you don't trust me, but I'm better than the stories about me.' The band has been stripped back, too. There's no brass section, and compared to the bombast and energised spirit of rehearsals, this seems almost low key. In between takes, he practises the line 'Winter, summer, spring, and fall, I'll be on the line waiting for your call.' Olly's so relaxed he forgets the iPhone bulging in his back pocket.

There are four takes. He occasionally fluffs his lines which prompts an outburst of mild swearing before he remembers the small production crew gathered for filming. 'Sorry for the rude words everyone,' he says.

Once *The Jonathan Ross Show* begins its recording later that evening, he settles on a sofa brimming with A-list quality – tripwire comedian, Russell Brand and movie star, Keanu Reeves. Brand seems pleased to see him.

'Olly, I've heard so many people say so many nice things about you that I feel I should shower you with kisses.'

Olly laughs. 'You can if you want...'

Before he has a chance to move, Brand has wrapped his arms around him. He's giving Olly's cheek a gentle peck.

TV host Ross is just as accommodating. He nudges Olly into talking about his recording career, an army of loyal fans and the family. He then lobs in a perennially hot bone of contention within the Murs camp: Olly's fractious relationship with his twin brother, Ben, who became estranged from the family when Olly was unable to attend his wedding due to *X Factor* commitments. The question bounces off him.

'That was ages ago,' he says. 'It was just a family thing. Unfortunately I couldn't make his wedding, so we had a falling out, yeah…'

Ross asks if the relationship has been repaired. In Olly's dressing room, Sarah is watching the show on a live feed. She sighs loudly. 'They bring this up every time.'

'No, it hasn't, no,' says Olly, giving very little away. 'It's still the same.'

The audience lets out a collective sigh of sympathy: 'Aahhh…'

'I know. It is sad, because he's part of the family, he's my twin.'

'That's a big thing,' says Ross.

Olly nods. 'More so for my mum and dad, because they've technically lost a son…'

Afterwards, he seems a little narked at being blindsided. There was no mention of the issue when Ross's production team presented him with the evening's proposed questions. Then Olly settles himself. He knows the game well enough not to take these issues too personally. 'People are cheeky like that – they always do it,' he says afterwards. 'To be fair, Jonathan has asked me about that before, so he probably thought to drop it in.'

Sarah reassures him, 'I thought you handled it well, babe.'

He bunkers down in the back of the Viano – an eight person people carrier – for the trip to Wakefield, and scrolls through his phone. Russell Crowe has messaged him on Twitter. 'Sorry about [missing you] young fella, am in Madrid now. Congratulations on all your success.' American record producer, Nile Rodgers, has also dropped him a note. Though Olly's more chuffed at the exchange of phone numbers that took place with Brand – 'He said, "If you're ever in trouble Murs, text me."'

He seems happy. Tomorrow is the first of four days in production rehearsals and he can regain some control. 'Performing: he's in his element,' says Sarah, as he drifts off to sleep. His headphones are on. Keanu Reeves's over-the-top action thriller, *Speed*, plays out on his phone – a movie about a bus journey on the brink of high drama.

OLLY ON THE RECORD: GETTING IN SHAPE FOR THE ROAD

People don't realise just how fit you have to be if you're going to perform on a massive arena tour. And it's not just about standing up there and singing either. I had to run around, dance and engage with the crowd. Even the adrenaline rush of playing in front of thousands of people was exhausting. It was also important that I didn't get sick, or become run down, because getting ill would have affected my voice and energy levels, and nobody wanted to put on a bad gig.

Because of all that I had to get seriously fit for the *Never Been Better* tour. I wanted to look good. I wanted to feel good. I wanted to be able to perform all my dance moves and not be out of breath between songs. I had been a little bit lazy in the years building up to it – I did some fitness, like cycling for Sport Relief and then training for the charity football match Soccer Aid, but I had to lose a little extra weight coming into this year. I had to change my diet and increase my fitness levels with my personal trainer, Rob. I loved the work but, bloody hell, it was hard at times.

Every morning we would do a bit of everything: strength-conditioning, cardio, boxing, circuits, press-ups and planks. When we hit the road, Rob came along with us and trained me pretty much every day – without wearing me out! It was amazing to have him along with us. He got me in great shape.

Being so fit wasn't a new experience for me. Before I started doing this job I was in shape for so many years and

I was at the peak of my fitness. I was a personal trainer before I did sales and recruitment, and I played football every week. Yeah, I was a lot younger then, but I remember feeling like I wanted to be fit. I ate well, I played well, I trained well. It was easier then. When I got into this life I learned that it isn't so easy to keep in shape, you don't always get the chance to train, what with all the travelling and performing. I've since managed to work out a good fitness regime for myself.

Chapter Three

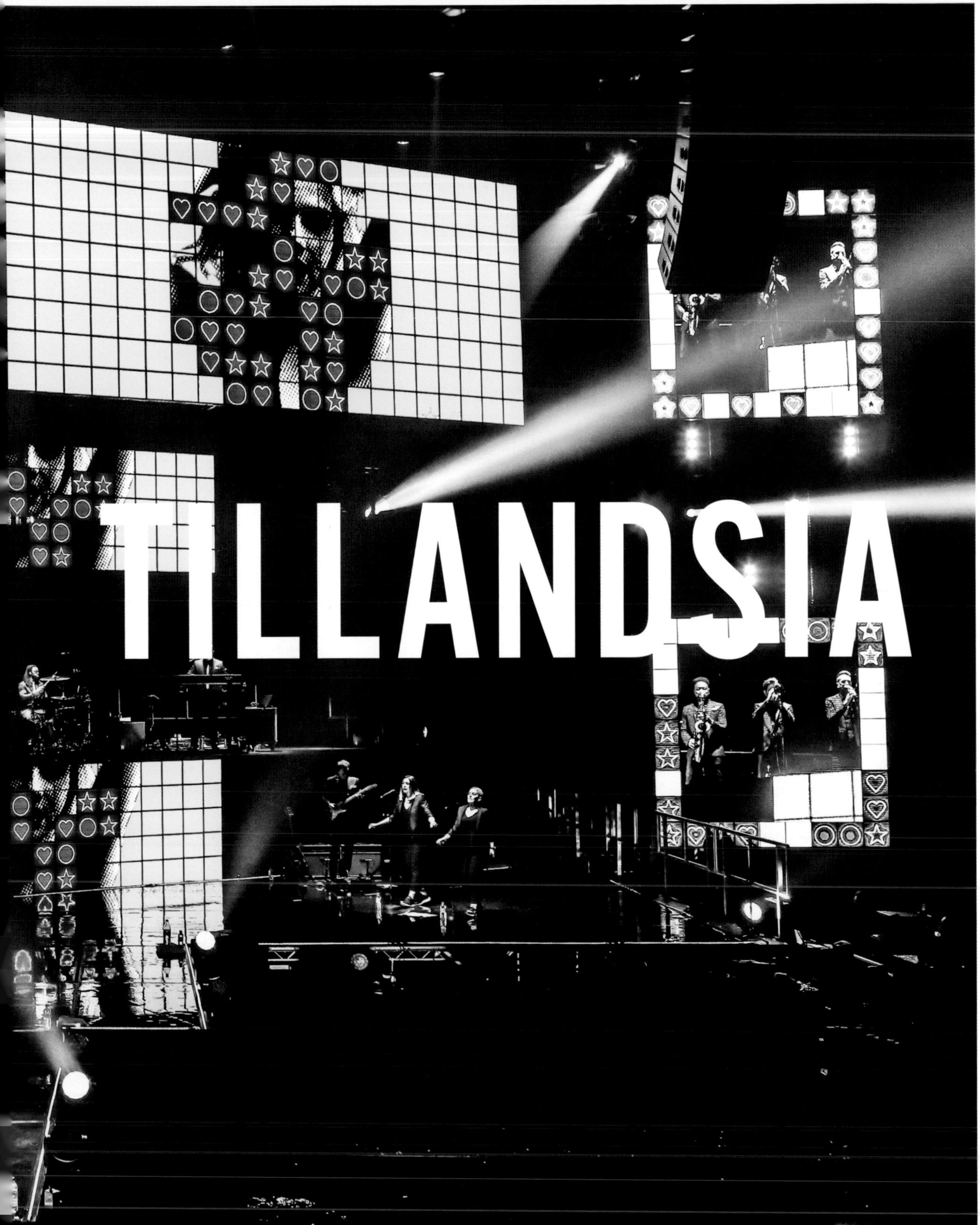

TILLANDSIA

TILLANDSIA

Three million quid goes a long way on the road. Olly's *Never Been Better* tour, a £2.9 million extravaganza, has been spread across 11 cities and 28 shows; there are 9 trucks of equipment and 51 permanent members of crew (plus 62 local roadies in every city on the schedule), providing catering, security, bus drivers, lights, stylists and hairspray, video equipment, tour programmes, merchandise and enough pyrotechnics to celebrate a royal anniversary.

Nearly all of it has been housed temporarily in LS-Live, a hangar-sized space in Wakefield. For the next few days, Olly and band, plus management, show producers and lighting directors, will tweak the live setlist constructed at SW19 studios into a fully functioning, arena-sized performance. The corridors are lined with photos of the facility's previous residents. Lavish stage shows by the likes of Paul Weller, The Prodigy, Westlife and Franz Ferdinand have all been schemed from this studio.

The tour's centrepiece for April and May is a vast black stage that rises out of the ground like a psychedelic battle cruiser. Bristling with strobing spotlights and neon strips, its glossy finish sparkles with reflected flares. Pinpoints of light ping across its surface via a bank of video screens that separate Olly from two storeys of band platform positioned at the back of the stage. It's from here that Sean and the musicians will run through the setlist to audiences of over 10,000 people. A runway-style catwalk extends into the crowd; designers have even dangled a movable stairway from the ceiling. At the flip of a switch it descends slowly, lights pulsing from every step. The ambitious, and slightly nerve-wracking, plan is for this 200-foot platform to connect Olly to another stage located at the back of nearly every venue on the tour. At key moments, he'll be able to walk above the heads of his audience as they crane their necks upwards from the seats below.

Olly hasn't seen it yet. He's still settling into his dressing room upstairs, a darkly lit living space complete with several luxurious mod cons. A portable games unit – effectively a large box on wheels, comprising his PlayStation console, Sonos speakers and TV – stands in the corner. There's a coffee table and one worn and inviting brown leather couch, big enough to sleep on. Black drapes and an antique, movie theatre-style spot-lamp bring a calming ambience to the soundproofed walls. It's quite the travelling lounge.

Olly drops his frame into the cushions, wriggling into a comfy, fetal position. 'I don't know about you, but I'm staying here and playing FIFA,' he says, reaching for a games pad. Much of his time on tour is spent in front of this screen, usually accompanied by Mark. It's an addictive presence at home, too. Getting mates round for a gaming session, he says, is a monthly occurrence – 'I'm not detached from reality. I'm firmly attached to it. I like to get the boys over.'

These marathon gaming stints are often accompanied by Olly's home-cooked sweet and sour chicken. 'And I'll still do my groceries. People stare at me in the supermarket like I've just landed from Mars, though. They'll go, "You do your own shopping?" But who else is gonna do it? I like to do the normal stuff, too.'

He's still happy to allow himself the occasional flash of Prince-style divadom however, should the opportunity present itself. A block of hollowed-out wood bark sits conspicuously on his coffee table. Covered in *Tillandsia* – or 'air plants' – it gives off a zesty fragrance. He cocks his head towards it. 'You been chopping down trees too, Ant?'

Ant Carr, production manager for the *Never Been Better* tour, is guiding Olly through the comforts set to fill his backstage space at every show. After each city shift, these assorted furnishings and fittings will be packed away and transported to the next venue on the schedule. The wood, says Ant, brings a nice fragrance to the room – 'Especially when rain water's sprinkled on the surface.' It's hard to tell whether he's yanking Olly's leg or not.

'It smells good,' says Olly, leaning in close. 'Really good. I like that. Looks nice around the place.'

Sarah pulls a face. She's also along for Ant's behind-the-scenes introduction to their touring infrastructure.

'Really, Olly?' she says. 'Oh, come on. You are not *that* artist.'

He laughs. 'Dunno, I could get used to this...'

There's work to be done here, too. Several boxes of tour programmes stand in the corner. Olly will have to sign around 2,000 copies for VIP guests before his tour comes off the road. These can wait for now. Today he's also due to walk the stage that will frame his voice for the next six weeks.

'Come on,' says Sarah, urging him up impatiently. 'Time for the big unveiling.'

He leaves his sofa with a groan, turns into the corridor and heads for a door marked 'Gallery Viewing', the seated section which looks down on his performance area. Ant stops him in his tracks.

'Whoa!' he shouts. 'Don't! You'll ruin the wow factor.'

Olly doesn't get it. 'But it's the best view in the house, isn't it?'

Sarah grabs the door handle before he can twist it open. 'No, it'll ruin the surprise.'

He seems a little confused. There's an expectant mood, like he's being treated to an extravagant Christmas present.

'Come on,' says Sarah. 'You need to see it from ground level first.'

He gives a reluctant nod, then walks through the production office, saying hello to the staff as he passes. He checks a tour book laying on a desk; a roll call of working crew, scanning its pages for any familiar names. But when Sarah opens the stage door, his focus changes. Through the frame, his stage cuts an imperious silhouette in LS-Live's cavernous rehearsal room – all angular edges, flashing beams and screens, and shiny black runways. Lights ricochet off every surface. Spiralling spot lamps scan the room. Olly takes it all in.

'Oh my god!' he says, checking the faces of Ant, Sarah and show producer, Elizabeth Honan. Elizabeth joins him with a kiss on the cheek and a hug. 'Oh... My... God. It's amazing, Beth.'

He steps closer. 'Wow. Wow. Wow!'

Closer still. He's laughing now.

'Bloody hell! The size of it.'

He pulls out his phone and takes pictures. One of the giant video screens flickers with static, an image slowly sharpening in the frame. It's the *Never Been Better* logo. Olly, dressed in a dapper, slim-fitting suit and tie, appears alongside it in fluro yellow and black. The digital form – a video shot some weeks back – leans into the camera. He's waving to what will be the audience below, urging them to cheer louder.

Ant is proudly talking through the work that went into construction – the stage design, its development, and the crew required to build it all. This labour arrived with an invoice for £200,000, apparently. But Olly's not listening. He's snapping more photographs and climbing the stage where Rupert, Louise and Katie are at their stations stage left; Sean above them, much higher, on a second level. Dexter, Mike, Kenji and Paul are stationed on the same platform. Ben is standing on the opposite wing with Darren and John. He's backed up against a honeycomb of bright light bulbs, rubbing his eyes, wincing.

'I turned around earlier and I think I've burned my retinas,' he says. 'I'm blinded.'

From the floor, Sarah watches as Olly moves from person to person, buzzing with hyped-up energy. He's like a kid with a shiny new toy.

'Scary,' she says. 'If that was me, I'd be freaked out going onto that stage for the first time. Thinking about what I had to do over the next couple of months would throw me. But he just seems... excited.'

Olly shouts down from the towering structure.

'Oi, Beth! It's like a bloody spaceship!'

—

Olly's back on his sofa. He's pondering the quirks of fate that made him one of the country's biggest pop stars. It's something that strikes him every time he walks onto a stage – 'I think, *I can't believe my luck*,' he says. 'It is strange. Every time, I have this moment where I go, *Bloody hell, this is bonkers*.'

The nuts and bolts of his success, he reckons, are pretty straightforward. 'There's not many people like me around, I guess,' he says. 'And Robbie Williams...'

What kind of people?

'You know, old school entertainers. We make the fans smile, people enjoy our shows. We have an easy way about us onstage. I'm not trying to be anyone else, I'm not trying to be Robbie, and it's just a natural thing.'

He reckons this easy stage manner first started taking shape before *X Factor*, when he watched the likes of Robbie, Michael Bublé, Michael Jackson and Justin Timberlake at home on TV – 'The people who inspired me to get up and dance when I was a kid growing up in Essex.'

He later stopped copying his heroes during karaoke and brought in some dance moves and jokes of his own making. 'It then got to a certain point in my life where I made the act mine. These days, it's me onstage. Olly Murs, not some tribute artist.'

Olly gets like this sometimes, especially when asked about his career. He's not chippy or arrogant, more defiant; confident, like there's a point still to prove about his creative worth. He often brings up the subject of work ethic in conversation. Like now. 'I've worked my arse off to get here,' he says this time. 'And I still do, pretty much every day.'

He attributes a little of this determined attitude to *X Factor*. The helping hand he received from the show has pigeon-holed him, he thinks – and for longer than expected, too. To some people he's still a reality TV show contestant, slugging it out to the supporters of Simon Cowell's global brand, rather than an artist in his own right. There's a gap of six years and four albums since his TV appearance, yet people still think of him as the runner-up from 2009. Sometimes it annoys him.

'The fact of the matter is, in plain and simple terms, anyone who comes from *X Factor* is given a tag,' he says. 'And it is a tag. You're from a reality TV show – from your own class. All the other artists, they're in a separate class.

'There's people constantly trying to dig out the guys from *X Factor*. There's always people out there saying we're not real songwriters, there's always people saying we're not real artists. It's not easy. It's a constant battle every year, but not a lot of people see it.'

As Olly recounts his frustrations, news of yesterday's meeting with *X Factor* is leaking into the press. By tomorrow morning it will be front page news.

—

He's under the stage now, standing on a 'man-lift' – a square platform designed to spring upwards quickly, revealing him at the front of the runway, somewhere in the thick of his audience. Above him, guitarist Rupert barrels through the choppy guitar riffs of 'Misirlou'. Images of Olly, dancing, flash across the giant screens again. He's pulling off his suit jacket, goading the audience into loud screams – louder. A checklist of greatest hits follows... 'Dear Darlin'... 'Never Been Better'... 'Troublemaker'... 'Seasons'... Then the countdown to show time... 10... 9... 8... 7... 6... 5... 4... 3... 2... 1!

Band cuts dead, house lights drop.

With a clunk of levers and pulleys, Olly is hoisted up onstage, dressed in black jeans, black trainers, grey jumper and just-rolled-off-the-sofa hair. For a moment he's motionless, fixed to the spot, arms by his side. A solitary spot lamp frames his silhouette. He takes a moment to survey the black, empty corners of the hangar. Next week, this will be an arena of 13,000 screaming people, but today he's making do with only a handful of road crew. He cups a hand to his ear,

listening to the imaginary adulation, soaking in a rowdy, party feel, though the only sound is an eerie clapping coming from somewhere below Olly's feet. It's Beth. She's guiding the show with stage directions pinned to a clipboard.

'OK, Olly, applause... applause... more applause... Hold...'

Mark is standing behind her. He lets out a loud chorus of boos.

Unfazed, Olly brings the microphone to his lips.

'Did you miss me?' he sings, an enquiring tone in his voice, cueing his band into the opening track from *Never Been Better*. He's sprinting around the stage, running from Darren and John on one side, to Katie and Louise on the other.

'What you been doing now that since I've been away? Have you felt good? Have you felt bad? Did you behave?' he sings, cat-walking down the runway stage. 'I could tell that you miss me, 'cause your eyes give it away. I know you can't resist me. So tell me, tell me, tell me, tell me, tell me girl, that you're listening... Oh!'

Olly skips backwards, trainers sliding across the glossy black floor, arms pointing at the empty shadows around him. He spins on the spot. There's a swift snap of heels, another verse.

Olly's stage front again now. 'Everyone!' he shouts. 'I'm back! I'm back!'

—

Beth wants Olly to strut more. He takes mouthfuls of lunch between staging suggestions as they discuss where he'll stand during songs. Other instructions include what to say to the crowd, and where his mic will be for every track – upstage, second floor, stage front; during a medley of early hits – 'Thinking Of Me', 'Busy' and 'Please Don't Let Me Go' – he'll be singing by a piano, surrounded by his backing vocalists as Sean plays keys. Beth suggests he lean into one of the TV cameras patrolling the stage edge during 'Why Do I Love You'. His image is due to be flashed up on the screens above him. During the close of 'Hand on Heart' there will be a quick breather – 'Olly will go offstage, have a little moment, towel himself down,' says Beth. Apparently he gets quite sweaty.

There's also a duet to coordinate. 'Up', Olly's top five single with Demi Lovato is set to be performed with tour support singer Ella Eyre, though she's not meeting with the band until opening night. Today, Louise has been drafted in as a temporary replacement. A tech positions two microphones side by side. Olly seems determined to enjoy the forced intimacy.

'I'm gonna make you as uncomfortable as I can for this performance, that OK, Louise?'

She smiles. 'Yeah, course. I've seen you in your boxer shorts already, so it's OK...'

Olly pretends to look awkward. He has, on occasion, wandered into the band dressing room in nothing but a pair of underpants. He pulls at his collar, laughing. 'Oh yeah, that's right. Don't tell my girlfriend, though.'

—

Back in the dressing room. Olly is explaining exactly why he decided to quit drinking on tour. The PlayStation helps to fill the downtime, he says, but he rarely parties after shows. The alcohol messes up his voice 'big time'. But he remembers the drinking days, back when he was finding his stage presence during those early pub shows with Small Town Blaggers, and later in his early personal appearances in the wake of *X Factor*. He would often hit the bar afterwards with 'the boys', or satisfied customers wanting to buy him a round. The results were always messy.

'My voice would fall apart the next day,' he says. 'The first time I did it, around the period when I'd finished *X Factor*, I thought, *Oh, this is a one off.* Then it happened again, so I decided to cut out the drinking on tour. Maybe the rest of the band think I'm a bit funny about drinking now, but I'm not. They're always surprised at the end of a tour when I get boozed up and they see that I can actually drink.

'Anyway, I'm quite a noisy person. I can't keep quiet, and with booze I start to shout. Then the voice goes...'

Mark walks in to deliver yet another box of tour programmes for Olly's signature. He's overheard the conversation.

'Yeah, he's right,' he says. 'Olly learned how to whisper in a helicopter.'

—

Another run through of the set.

Olly finishes the acoustic weepy, 'Let Me In', an album track taken from *Never Been Better* and written with rock institution, Paul Weller – the pair first met at a Paolo Nutini gig where they agreed to sketch out a song together. Today, he delivers its final chorus sitting down. His legs dangle from the edge of the stage.

'See, if I was rock'n'roll, this is the point where I'd have a whiskey and a fag,' he says, sucking on an imaginary smoke. 'But I'm not, I'm a mummy's boy.'

—

The only thing bothering him as he travels back to the hotel in the people carrier, with Sarah, Mark and Sean, is the scissor lift. A moveable platform, it rises 15 feet during the encore of 'Wrapped Up', pushing him high above the audience. It looks a little wobbly. Sarah raises her concerns when Olly mentions it – 'Oh my god...'

He knows what's coming next. 'Don't say it.'

'But my heart stopped, I thought you were going to fall off.'

He sighs. 'I kept thinking, *It's gonna break, I'm falling backwards.* It's not the nicest place to be, I'm not gonna lie. It doesn't feel that safe up there, but it's a big area and I'm not moving from the middle.'

He gives a shrug. 'At the end of the day, if it falls, it falls. I'd have died doing something that I loved – in action. Anyway, there's a Madame Tussauds waxwork of me out there in Blackpool now. They'll remember me.'

—

'They' are waiting for him outside the hotel; a small gang of fans stationed here since the early afternoon. It's nine o'clock in the evening and Wakefield, observes Olly, is not the warmest place in March. The girls – all of them are girls – look cold. Olly recognises their faces, but rather than being pleased to see him they're as surly as you would expect anyone to be, having stood in a cold car park for several hours.

'Oh, give us a smile,' shouts Mark, leaning out of the window. Most of the crew are on nodding terms with these fans, such is their regularity at tour locations like this one.

One of them forces a sarcastic grin.

'Alright?' she says, sulkily, as Olly gets out of the car to say hello. They've met countless times before, and she's always eager to grab a selfie with him, but her mood is a little mardy.

Sarah understands this dance all too well. Often it takes place in hotel bars and foyers, where hardcore fans regularly gather to grab pictures with Olly when he returns from shows, or rehearsals. It's not just teenagers, either. One of the girls here talks about her husband at home. Sarah knows that he'll sign autographs for all of them. He's happy to natter away, no matter where he has to be or what he has to do.

'Come on, hug him,' shouts Mark, getting impatient with the delay. He's arranged a band meeting, a welcoming get together that precedes every tour Olly does. 'Quick picture, come on!'

The girls want to talk about the show, what he'll be playing, but the time he's willing to share has run out. Olly gives them all a kiss, poses for photos and thanks them for hanging around. He's always gracious for the support, but he knows this is the strange flipside to his fame – the fans waiting around for autographs and photos, even though they've already met him on countless occasions already; the girls obsessing over his lyrics and album releases at home, who then act moodily when he turns up.

'Thanks girls!' he shouts, diving back into the van, sliding the door behind him. He's out of earshot now. 'Bloody hell, that lot can be grumpy sometimes,' he says, waving out of the window. 'But I love them. I've known them for five years, they've been there from the beginning, and they've never changed.'

The hotel is discreet enough, away from Wakefield's town centre and set back in a country lane. Mark's not taking any chances, though. He's booked a function room for his meeting, to keep some privacy. Everyone is involved – band, plus Sarah, Mark, tour security Tony Murphy (Mark's brother), personal driver Paddy and tour assistant Jordan Thomas.

As everyone orders drinks, Mark gets up and pulls the group together. He welcomes the new faces – Kenji, Dexter, Katie and Louise – and delivers a stern warning to everyone not to lose their itineraries, the detailed tour dossier of travel times and hotel bookings. It's secret info he doesn't want falling into the wrong hands. 'All my months of planning will go out of the window if it does,' he says. 'The fans will be everywhere.

'Oh, and just on a social media point of view, remember backstage is backstage. It's for the band, it's for Olly, I just don't wanna see people tweeting pictures. It's about having a bit of privacy. We've got a green room for everyone to hang out in, a fun environment, and we want to keep it like that. The public gets to see Olly from the front of the stage, they don't need to see anything from the back.'

Olly stands up. It looks as if he's about to make an important announcement. Instead the speech turns out to be a terrible gag. 'I just want to say, always remember… Nah, it's gone. Have a good one!'

He sits down quickly. 'I stole that joke from someone,' he admits, though he can't remember from whom. As everyone begins to chat and gossip he mentions Dermot O'Leary. Apparently, one of tomorrow's papers is announcing his decision to leave *X Factor*. The bookies' odds on Olly getting the job are 2/1, reckons Mark.

Olly leans in. 'Seriously? I might have a bet on myself.'

It's not long before his first drink is finished. Olly orders another. Someone hooks their phone into the room's speaker system and before long a party atmosphere kicks in. It's a cue for Olly to unwind. There is a buzz about him now. His tour begins in two days. The novelty of rehearsals is wearing off. He wants to perform in front of real crowds, real fans.

'I'm more excited than nervous,' he says. 'I can't wait to stand out there. In rehearsals, you're basically performing to a wall. It's very hard as a performer. It's not the same as it is playing in front of your own fans who love your music.' He knows the show won't be perfect for the first few nights. There's bound to be glitches and a short period of tweaking, maybe even some setlist changes. 'I'll just chat and wing it with the crowd between songs,' he says.

He shouts out to Sean, who's currently single – or a 'single Pringle', as he calls it. 'Go into that wedding next door and say, "There's three guys in here who are available." Not me though.'

Sarah doesn't look impressed. 'You want to invite that whole wedding in here?' she says.

Mark laughs. 'Remember those two rehearsals we're doing tomorrow? It's now the one.'

OLLY ON THE RECORD: THE FANS

My fans are great, the *greatest*, and they've got me to where I am today. As soon as the live shows started on *X Factor*, they kept on voting for me, week after week, until I got to the final. Then they bought my records as soon as I signed a deal. Since then, they've helped me to pack out arenas up and down the country. The love and support blows my mind sometimes.

They're everywhere I go. I appreciate that now and I always look forward to seeing them when I'm on the road, but in the early days... wow, it freaked me out. I kept asking Mark and Sarah, 'How do people find out? How do they know where I'm staying, where I'm going to eat?' After a while I got my head around it all.

Not long after I started playing live shows, I went on tour with One Direction, and that helped. It's when I really got a taste of how tricky it can be for some people. It was a couple of years back and there were hundreds of 1D fans outside every hotel. It didn't matter what city we were in, the fans were there every day. It was on a much bigger and more intense scale, so I know what I'm experiencing isn't that bad.

These days I understand that my fans are going to follow me around whenever I go on tour, and that they can suss out where I'm going to be. Some of these guys have been doing it for years, and with social media like Twitter and Facebook, they can easily alert everyone about where I'm staying. It only takes one tweet and the news is out about where I am. Straight away, there are 50 people outside my hotel.

The good news is that my fans are respectful – they always have been. They don't sneak onto my hotel floor, or knock on my door while I'm sleeping.

They don't ring me at midnight. Once they get their picture taken with me or they've got an autograph, and we've said hi, they go home.

I've got to know some of them over the years because they've been around so much. There are even organised fan groups like 'The Olly Murs Girls' and 'The A Team'. Then there are the fans that come along on every tour – like Brooke and Lozza. They've been supporting me from day one. I suppose, in the end, you almost feel like they're mates. I can't stop every time to chat with them because I'm so busy, but they know that I will when I can.

The thing about all of this is, no matter what you've done, no matter how great your album sounds, or how brilliant you think you are onstage, it means nothing until the fans are there in front of you. I could do the best show in the world, but if the fans aren't around to dance to the songs, it doesn't matter.

They keep me on my toes, too. For as long as I'm performing, I have to keep evolving as an artist – for them. I'm not going to stop making music, but I can only put on tours and record albums for as long as people want me to carry on. Plus, I know there's a sell-by date for every artist. I'm not sure what my sell-by date will be, but I want to make sure that I'm progressing all the time. I want the next album to be better than the last. That way I can continue seeing those fans on the road.

Chapter Four

THE 'X FACTOR SHOPPING EXPERIENCE'

THE 'X FACTOR SHOPPING EXPERIENCE'

Olly has chartered a helicopter. It's one of the perks of being a multimillionaire pop star on the verge of a UK tour, where even the simplest of travel plans can become problematic. And so it proves 24 hours before *Never Been Better*'s opening night in Sheffield. With production rehearsals finished for the weekend, and his band travelling to a hotel near the venue, Olly must fly across the Pennines with Sarah, Mark and Tony for the unveiling of his Madame Tussauds waxwork in Blackpool. It's agreed that a long bus journey will be too tiring for him today, especially given the workload of rehearsals, tomorrow's gig, and the hype aligned to a red carpet reveal of his sculptured lookalike.

'It'll be too long a day if we go by bus,' he says to Sarah. He's nestling into his seat at the back of the people carrier. 'It was fine on tours before, because I'd be working on pure adrenaline, pure excitement. I couldn't believe I was doing a tour. Remember that? I was like a Duracell Bunny, running around everywhere. There wasn't an off button.'

The team is heliport-bound, though the designated landing pad actually comprises a couple of grassy acres in a Wakefield farm. On the back seat of the car there's some excited chatter about the idea of an end-of-tour boxing competition. Olly wants to 'batter' Mark and Tony. Both of them measure up at over six feet in height and 16 stone.

'Two hits' says Mark. 'One hit to the head, the second when you hit the ground.'

'I don't know about this, Olly,' says Sarah, turning up her nose. 'Are you going to wear head guards? I don't want you doing your European shows with a smashed-in face.'

He shrugs. 'Hashtag: *Whatevs*.'

Olly's phone has been buzzing with messages all morning. Everyone wants to know if he's taking the *X Factor* job. The papers have discovered that both he and Caroline Flack are being lined up for the presenting roles in the revamped version of the show. 'Dermot's cool with everything,' he tells Sarah. 'I've spoken to him.'

It pings again. This time it's radio host, Chris Evans: 'Congrats on the *X Factor* job!' The former Radio One DJ is receiving similar press headlines to Olly; following Jeremy Clarkson's departure from *Top Gear* after an 'unprovoked physical and verbal attack' on one of the show's producers, a number of stories have tipped him as favourite to front the motoring show.

Olly laughs. 'I should tell him, "Congrats on the Top Gear job, mate..."'

Despite his animated mood, there are some nerves. His chosen mode of transport today, like Beth's scissor lift, is giving him the jitters a little. As the people carrier pulls up at its destination, he eyes the chopper nervously.

'I don't like flying,' he admits. He's shedding anything remotely heavy from his bag, iPad included. 'I don't want to weigh that thing down.'

Olly gives the driver a hug as he gets out. 'Have a good show tomorrow night,' he laughs. 'Just in case.'

He buckles himself into his seat. As the blades above his head begin to whirr, he drops the bulky in-flight headphones onto his lap. Olly's worried that wearing them during the journey might leave a dent in his voluminous, swept-back quiff. Which would be annoying, given that his hair has been styled to look just like his Madame Tussauds model – the very same model that's been styled to look just like him.

—

Chartering aircraft for a Madame Tussauds unveiling is considered unusual, even by pop star standards. Gwen Stefani – lead singer with American rock band, No Doubt and judge for the US version of TV show, *The Voice* – previously had been the only musician to drop in from the sky; her grand arrival came with a private jet to the museum's Vegas branch. Olly's entrance is a little less extravagant today: Blackpool's seen-better-days seafront is in the middle of a storm. Rain lashes the promenade and windy gusts yank plastic bags high into the air. This hasn't stopped a couple of hundred fans, here to catch a brief glimpse of Olly, from standing in the wintry conditions for several hours.

'Bloody hell,' he says, peering at the crowd. A people carrier has collected him from Blackpool's private airport and is driving him along the seafront. 'They've been here all day in this?'

He then spots a discount outlet on the high street called the 'X Factor Shopping Experience' – 'Everything for a fiver? *Hilarious*.'

He's excited about seeing his likeness, but the waxwork's baggy eyelids are still bothering him – 'Do you think they make me look older?' he says, scanning the picture on his phone again. A representative from Madame Tussauds sits alongside him. He's wearing a shirt unbuttoned, somewhat disconcertingly, to his navel. As the people carrier approaches the museum, he talks excitedly about the importance of Olly's waxwork model.

'We only add three a year,' he says. 'The comedian, John Bishop and Paddy McGuinness from *Take Me Out* are the other two for 2015...'

But Olly's not listening. His mum, Vicky, has texted. She's already arrived at the museum, along with dad, Pete, and they've caught an early glimpse of his likeness. He reads out their message to the car: 'Just bumped into you, but you're not very talkative...'

Olly laughs. 'She's used to seeing double, she's had two of me before,' he says, making reference to his twin brother, Ben.

What follows during the next five minutes is a well-rehearsed procession, one that's become increasingly chaotic as his fame has intensified over the years. The people carrier draws into the curb and the door is pulled open to high-pitched screams from the crowd. Flashlights blink. Mark and Tony jump out first, followed by Olly. There are louder yells. Teenage girls lean over crash barriers, waving posters, CD artwork and magazines – his image across the front.

Smartphones are waved in his face as security guards watch for any grabbing hands; Mark holds an umbrella above Olly's head. As well as his safety, there's an expertly groomed quiff to protect from the rain. Olly signs everything thrust his way and stoops for selfies. Not everyone gets to see him, though. As he walks the red carpet, those stuck at the back of the crowd become hysterical.

'Olly!'

'Olly, don't go... Please don't go!'

There are louder screams. 'Olly!'

Louder still. *'OLL-EEEEEE! PLEEEEEEASE!'*

He stops briefly to pose for press photographers at the doors, and a mic is handed to him so he can address the crowd. His speech only lasts 15 seconds – a hello, a big thanks to the fans – but it's impossible to hear anything through the din. One fan, only metres away, repeatedly screams his name at full volume.

She's reaching out to grab him, her face reddening with every yell. She's so noisy that his exit into the eerie silence of Madame Tussauds' 'Big Night In' exhibition provides a moment of relative serenity.

'Bloody hell, a bit mad out there, innit?' says Olly, in a grand understatement.

He's ushered through a holding area full of fans – winners of a meet and greet competition – and into the press room, where the model is standing on a small stage, his name emblazoned across the backdrop. There are TV cameras and presenters too, some local newspaper journalists. Vicky and Pete are waiting for him. He gives them both a hug.

'It's better looking than you,' says Pete.

They all stand back and admire the likeness. Its quiff has been suitably uplifted, and the skin tones now match his post-sunbed glow. Olly: v2.0's eyelids are still a little baggy, though.

'Can you see Dad in him?' says Olly, nudging Vicky and pointing to the blemish on the synthetic cheek. 'It's the Murs' mole...'

Sarah suggests they pull in close for a selfie, their arms around the wax figure. Olly grabs the crotch and gives an approving wink. 'It's the hardest I've been for a while,' he laughs. Vicky pulls a face as several photographers gather round to take shots. On request, Olly hugs his model, scratches the stubble on its chin and shapes to land a right hook on the jaw. Somebody asks if he'd like to give himself a kiss.

'Nah,' says Vicky under her breath, now standing on the sidelines. 'He'll get ripped for that... I'd kiss it though.'

She's not a fan of the press attention. The family has been stung by snooping journalists and negative headlines too many times in the past. 'We realised how dirty they can be when journalists came round to ours one day, asking questions about our son, Ben's wedding and I said, "We don't wanna talk to you." They went straight round to Pete's mum's and said, "Vicky's just sent us here and said you wouldn't mind having a chat." She let them in. I realised from that day that you do not trust the press.'

Has that made you more paranoid?

'Totally. It's the only thing I don't like about it. I'm a private person. What Olly says and does is fine, but if we get dragged into it...'

But they've since learned that the positives of Olly's fame have far outweighed the bad – the gigs, meeting the likes of Robbie Williams and Madness, and travelling the world are all plus points. 'What he's done for us, we can't take that away from him,' she says. 'He's been a great son.'

A crowd of journalists begin to ask questions. Granada TV are first.

'Well, Olly Murs,' says the presenter, 'after four months, your wax figure is complete. What's your reaction?'

Olly smiles. 'I'm shocked. I dunno, it's a strange feeling.'

He steps back and admires the model again. The presenter asks him about the design process. 'They get all your measurements to make it realistic,' he says. '*They go everywhere*.'

Does he like it? 'I've got to say, I like his hair. But I've lost a lot of weight since it was made. I'm amazed... It's a very proud moment for me and my family.'

As with press junkets of this kind, a pre-emptive round of gentle questioning represents an unwritten contract between media and event organisers. In exchange for celebrity access, a newspaper or TV station must name-check whichever brand has invited them in. These polite trade-offs are usually dealt with very quickly, especially when there's a bigger issue to discuss... like today. With the diplomatic questioning out of the way, what everyone really wants to know is whether there's any truth in the *X Factor* rumour.

'So, Dermot has left,' says the presenter. 'You're kind of in the pipeline – you and Caroline Flack. What have you got to say about it? Is it true?'

'It's just rumours,' says Olly. 'Just rumours. But I'll let the papers speculate.'

He'd like to move on, to talk about something else, but she's not letting go. 'Is it a job you'd want to do?'

'I've presented on the show before with *Xtra Factor*, I loved it with Caroline, but the music is my focus and I've got a tour to look forward to.'

A *Daily Mirror* reporter asks if he's talked to Dermot about his departure.

'Can we talk about the waxwork?' says Olly, getting a little exasperated.

'They're just rumours…'

'But would you like to do it, though?'

He begins to repeat himself, using the age-old trick of filling newspaper paragraphs with obvious statements, harmless sound bites and platitudes; the art of talking a lot while saying very little. It's a routine long perfected by Premier League footballers and red-carpeting Hollywood stars. 'It's a lot of rumours,' he says. 'Me and Caroline worked together years ago. There's always speculation – every year.'

He turns on the charm again. 'Listen, with this, I'm here in Blackpool forever,' he says, gesturing to the model. 'You can't get rid of me now. The Essex boy has landed.'

Another *X Factor* question is put to him. Then another. A representative from Madame Tussauds calls time on the interview. 'One last question. Madame Tussauds only, please…'

The silence is deafening. Press conference over.

—

Olly, Vicky and Pete are recalling the first time his celebrity became an issue for the family. It was around the screening of his third or fourth appearance on *X Factor*. Olly was home, relaxing, when his mum sent a text. The family was in a Chelmsford shopping centre. They hadn't seen each other for a little while, what with him being so busy. Did he fancy meeting them?

Olly wasn't so sure. Going into a busy high street might be tricky, he figured, what with all the tabloid attention building around him, so he tried to put the meeting off. 'Mum, I really want to see you,' he replied, 'but if I go into Starbucks, it'll be a nightmare.' Vicky wasn't having it, though. The boys in the family needed to buy some suits for his sister's wedding.

'So I caved in,' says Olly. 'I thought, *OK let's see how this plays out*. And for the first few minutes it was alright. Then somebody asked for a photo. There was another request a bit later, and then another. People wanted autographs. Eventually it was like the whole cafe had come around us at our table.'

Vicky hated it. 'We didn't know what to do, we just weren't used to it. Looking back it was the worst thing we could have done, wasn't it? My poor mum was with us and she was in a wheelchair. This queue appeared. It was going out of the coffee place and into the road. People were climbing over my mum to get to him, and Olly's sister Faye shouted, "Get off my nana!"'

A scene followed. An overeager parent started pushing and shoving.

'Do you mind?' shouted Vicky. 'I'm having a coffee with my son!'

The fan didn't care. 'Well, I'm with my daughter,' she said. 'And I want to get an autograph right now.'

Vicky explains how Olly calmed the situation down and stopped things from turning ugly, but it was a lesson for everyone. 'I think Mum understood what was happening after that,' he says.

Had your life changed forever?

'Yeah, especially with us,' says Vicky. 'You're on *X Factor* and you get people to vote; they put you on the show, then it's all over and you're left. You're just put out there. Afterwards, you have people knocking on your door, the press, cars

coming past the house – we call them Olly drive-bys. We've lost a little bit of our identity really. We're not Vicky and Pete anymore.'

Pete agrees. Recently a friend of his had a T-shirt printed up for him as a present. On the front it read, 'Olly's Dad: Formerly Known As Peter Murs'.

—

Olly reckons that he doesn't have 'that' kind of relationship with his parents, one where he feels he should call home every day. He doesn't feel the need to fill them in on every detail of his life on the road. Twitter can take care of that, after all. 'They know if anything happened, or if I was going through something, if it was serious enough, I'd ring them,' he says.

There were times in his life when they were worried for him, though. In 2008, Olly was working in a call centre. He decided to quit his job and travel Australia for a few months. When he returned to Essex he told them that he wanted to take another stab at an *X Factor* audition, even though he had failed twice previously. They thought he was crazy.

'Remember that, Pete?' says Vicky. 'At the time it was like, "Eh? You're 25, you need to get yourself settled into something – a job, marriage, the usual thing you do." That's what we were trying to steer him towards. But he was like, "Nah, I'm gonna do this again, I'm gonna try *X Factor*." He winds me up about it now. He says, "If I'd listened to you, Mum..." But he wouldn't have listened to me anyway.'

Pete nods. 'Olly said that he just wanted to get in front of the judges properly. He wanted to get in front of Simon Cowell for him to say, "No."'

Olly remembers there were a few arguments about his decision. 'I always said, "It's not about being an artist, or a pop star. I just want to be involved in music – any sort of music. I don't care if I'm onstage in front of thousands of people, or if I'm working as a crew guy, I just wanna be involved. I wanna be a music teacher, I wanna entertain kids. I wanna be at Butlins. Any of it, just as long as I'm involved."'

Their concerns weren't surprising, considering. Olly's upbringing had been pretty normal up until that point; he was hardly the superstar-in-waiting type. Sure, they knew he could sing, he could entertain the family, but those gigs with

Small Town Blaggers weren't exactly The Big Time. Nobody knew of him outside of a karaoke pub in Witham. 'We could see he had talent and a dream, though,' says Pete. 'But as a parent, you wanna see your son get a career. You wanna see him get his feet firmly on the ground.'

When it came to his first appearance on *X Factor*, Vicky and Pete couldn't go. They had already promised to see his sister in Surrey that day, they said, and wouldn't be able make the filming of his studio audition. Their dog, Molly, was left at home. It was Olly's job to walk her when he returned from his audition.

'We were waiting for him to ring up, to let us know that he was home, that he was letting the dog out,' says Vicky. 'Then he calls and said, "Guess what? I've got through." I just thought, *Wow!* The dog must have been cross-legged, poor thing. Simon Cowell loved her when he came round a while later for some filming, didn't he? He picked her up and then she peed all down him. Molly must have thought, *Simon Cowell! Pssssst!* How embarrassing...'

—

He feels guilty when he hasn't seen his mates and the family a for while – when he's on tour, or away working – so he treats them. 'Not with gifts or anything like that,' he says. 'I'm not showing off with my money, but I might take everyone out for a meal, or get my friends around for drinks at the end of a tour.'

His sister always tells him that she doesn't want presents. 'I just want you to come round for a cuppa more often,' she says.

—

Olly chats to his parents for a while and meets the fans. He kisses a queue of girls and poses for more selfies.

'He hasn't changed,' says Vicky. 'He's still exactly the same. He's not any different to what he was when he was a lad. Since he was a baby, really. He's just Oliver – what you see is what you get.'

Pete reckons it's because his son found fame at a relatively older age. 'He came to it as an adult, not a teenager who wanted to be a star with no life skills. Olly already had the life skills. Like with money. He knew that if he wanted the best wallet to show the girls that he was a bit flash, he had to buy the wallet first. Then he'd have to wait a few weeks until he could earn the money to put in it. He had a Gucci wallet once – it cost him about £150. It was a couple of weeks before he had any cash to fill it up with, but that was Olly.'

'To be honest with you, I don't think we'd let him change,' says Vicky. 'We'd kick his backside. If he ever had a diva strop, we'd clip him around the earhole.'

She recalls an earlier conversation, during which Olly had moaned about her ringing him on tour. He'd said she was 'too intense'. Vicky had bristled.

'I said, "I'll give *you* intense. I'll be ringing you up every day next week."'

There are posters to be signed, but with a helicopter waiting for his return, time is running short. Mark's keen to get him to the next hotel on his itinerary. Before he leaves, there's one last picture opportunity. Olly's spotted the popular Madame Tussauds *X Factor* exhibit. A scowling, ghoulish-looking Simon Cowell, dressed in what looks like a grey schoolteacher's jumper, sits on one side, and

Louis Walsh the other. He hands Sarah the phone and poses in the empty chair positioned between the two judges. As she grabs a few shots, the potentially disastrous implications of his stunt begins to sink in.

'God, whatever you do, Olly, don't put this on Instagram,' she says.

—

Photographs and TV interviews completed, Olly can wear his headphones for the helicopter ride to Sheffield. By joking and messing around with an attached system microphone, he's able to treat the accompanying passengers to an intimate sing-song. He begins his show with a verse from 'Seasons' – 'Baby girl with the broken smile, would you mind if you stayed awhile'. It's followed by the rousing chorus from 'Right Place Right Time'– 'I'm hanging on for dear life, hoping we can make this a long night'. He calls his a cappella rendition 'Murs FM'.

A voice cuts through his harmonies. It's the pilot.

'I think I preferred our first flight... When I couldn't hear you,' he says.

OLLY ON THE RECORD: GETTING PRANKED BY ANT AND DEC

While I was getting my waxwork put together, Ant and Dec decided to prank me for their TV show, *Saturday Night Takeaway*. At the time, I'd been asked to go in for what would be my '3D scanning' at the Madame Tussauds HQ. I was told this session was all part of the creative process, and a step that everyone lucky enough to get a likeness made of them has to go through – it ensures that every model looks as realistic as possible. What I didn't know was that there was no such technique. Everything was already in place for my wax clone to be completed, and instead a trap had been laid.

When I arrived at the Madame Tussauds studio, everybody in the building was in on the gag – except me. God knows how my manager was able to keep it a secret. Once I'd arrived, every step I took seemed to be hampered by some little cock-up or another. At first, I got into a lift with this weird bloke who smelled a bit funny (that was Ant in disguise, by the way). The elevator then stopped on every floor, which was pretty uncomfortable given the stink, and, at one point, a waxwork of Michael Jackson even joined us. That blew my mind. All I could think was, *Wow, that looks so cool.*

Once we got into their offices, I was told that I had to wear a fetching coloured pair of tight pants so the team could get my body shape exactly right. (Quick footnote: if you do watch the clip on YouTube, please bear in mind that a. tight pants aren't the most

flattering of outfits, and b. it was a cold day). I was then put in a weird booth for them to do the scans, which was when the fun and games really began. The electrics went *bang!* and sirens started going off. The machine seemed to be short-circuiting, and I tried to get out, but the door was locked. That's when loads of gunge started squirting from one of the panels inside, covering me from head to toe.

Believe it or not, the penny only started to drop at that moment. I was like, *Gunge coming from a machine? That can't be right...* Up until that point I'd been completely sucked in, so when I saw Ant and Dec coming towards me all I could think was, *You bastards! I've been shafted...*

I guess you could consider being pranked by those two a bit of an honour these days. They're TV royalty in the UK, after all. But while the laughing was going on, I must admit, I felt a little bit worried. For a second, I figured that maybe the honour of my becoming a Madame Tussauds waxwork had been a prank as well. Luckily, that wasn't the case at all. The Essex Boy is now a tourist attraction in Blackpool – for now, at least.

Chapter Five

FEEL LIKE FUNKIN' IT UP

FEEL LIKE FUNKIN' IT UP

It's the morning before Olly's first night on the *Never Been Better* tour. He has trained in the hotel gym and steamed his throat, a restorative process that will soothe any aches and strains caused by those four days in rehearsals. Other precautionary measures are in place, too. He drinks cups of hot water with honey and lemon. Whenever Mark stops by Olly's hotel room, he complains about the high temperatures. As a singer, he finds that air conditioning can make his larynx 'a bit scratchy'. Clearly nothing's taken for granted in the run-up to the big show.

Meanwhile Mark has emailed a call sheet to the touring party – an itinerary of obligations and important not-to-be-missed events, such as the band's onstage time. Olly's timetable is punctuated with moments of personal space, an hour or two in which he can relax, take some time for himself, and become reacquainted with his PlayStation console. It's a window that Mark calls 'FIFA time', a reference to Olly's favourite football game.

13.00 – Lunch
13.30 – FIFA Time
15.00 – Vocal Warm-ups
15.30 – Soundcheck
16.15 – FIFA Time
17.00 – Grooming
17.30 – Photo in Dressing Room for the Sun *(casual/not groomed)*
17.45 – Hallam FM Radio Interview

18.00 – Dinner
19.00 – FIFA Time
20.00 – Grooming
20.45 – Time to show your fans what they have been missing! Did they miss you? [sic] *Hell Yeah, Bring It!!!!*

—

Olly walks backstage, ignoring the vast banks of seats that go on forever in the Motorpoint Arena Sheffield – back, back, back, and up, up, up. He steps past

walls of flight cases, mixing desks and catering equipment. His dressing room is positioned somewhere beyond the offices where a seemingly endless diary of tour commitments – meet and greets with fans, guest tickets, interviews with the local press – are being organised. This will be his home for the next five weeks: the backstage corridors that look the same in every venue, the mobile canteens, the showers, the toilets, the sport dressing rooms converted into functional office spaces. Such is the disorientating uniformity of his touring life – hotel, backstage, FIFA time, grooming, interviews, meet and greet, gig; over and over – that he often loses track of the days. The confusion is such that Olly sometimes has to remind himself of the host cities and venues where he is playing.

'The first thing I'll shout to them tonight is, "Hello Sheffield!"' he says. 'It sounds ridiculous, but I make sure I know the place I'm in. It's drummed into my head: today I'm in Sheffield.' He hasn't got a city wrong yet when touring, but as he gets deep into this tour, he knows his daily routine will become even more confusing.

On the first night, though, there will be one or two mistakes. Experience has taught him that songs in the early performances are often moved around, or tweaked. Maybe they'll be edited out altogether. It happens with every tour and he's fine with it – just as long as he remembers where he is tonight.

'I'm in Sheffield,' he repeats. 'Hello, Sheffield... What's going on, Sheffield? How you doing, Sheffield?'

Recalling performances in different cities helps him, too; it sharpens his connection to a show. Tonight should be easy enough. The last time Olly was here, there was that embarrassing incident with his torn trousers.

'I spread my legs and they ripped. *Bang!* My crown jewels popped out,' he laughs. 'Might have to mention that...'

Even his dressing room adds to the uniformity – it's identical to the lounge space that played home during those production rehearsals in Wakefield. The black drapes; his sofa, spot lamp and games console are all in place. Ant's *Tillandsia* still smell nice. Olly settles in for the afternoon and switches on the game console. It's FIFA time.

Despite the 13,000 tickets sold for the opening gig, and a string of sell-outs beyond, he's still in an unflustered mood. 'If we'd put this tour on and no one was turning up, then I'd be worried,' he says. 'Before the show had even started I'd be bricking it.' The pressure doesn't worry him. Nor does the fact that tonight there's going be a host of key management figures analysing the show: Modest! are in attendance, as are tour promoters, his agent, record label representatives and radio pluggers, plus a guest list of reviewing journalists and photographers.

He hasn't always been this relaxed. When touring first began in the wake of his *X Factor* success, Olly's early shows were racked with nerves and insecurity. 'I used to panic about it.' He didn't enjoy his early gigs half as much as he does now. 'Because it was all new to me. It was different, every night. There was a pressure to perform in front of everyone. Now I enjoy every second, every minute.'

There were other stresses, too. Whenever he was invited to play club shows, Mark would drive him to the venue. When they returned to his car they'd find that somebody – a jealous boyfriend, usually – had scratched a key through the paintwork. As Olly kicks back for the afternoon, Tony stands outside his door. 'I don't usually walk around with security,' he says. 'And I get a bit uncomfortable when he's there, but sometimes I need him.'

—

He pops out for lunch, to chat with Mark and Sarah, to sit with his band mates. Katie asks him whether his girlfriend, Francesca, will be here tonight. Olly shakes his head.

'Nah, I told her I don't want her to come yet because the show's not ready.'

Apparently Francesca was a little put out at first.

'But, I'm your girlfriend,' she'd said. 'I want to be there.'

He told her that there would be mistakes, that he'd rather she came after a couple of weeks, when the show was running smoothly. 'I'm not even letting my mum and dad come over until then, either.'

But she's cool about it now. 'From her perspective she wants to see me and spend time with me. And being in a relationship, we need that. But on the flip side, it's about getting the balance right, so I've said she can come to the cities where I've got time off during the week, and then we can have a couple of days together. If I didn't see her for the whole five or six weeks, it would be a nightmare.'

—

The *Sun* newspaper is one of several publications here to interview Olly; showbiz reporter Dan Wootton has been dispatched to deliver the questions. He asks Olly about the *X Factor* rumours, the passing of his nan ('It's obviously really sad for us as a family,' he says), and his relationship with Francesca. 'I think the missus was a little bit worried I was losing this weight. She's been stuffing me up for the last two years, haha! But I've got to look good for the ladies!'

He points out that Olly is a well-behaved boyfriend.

'We added two female singers to the band this time, but I drew the line at getting a load of female dancers in as well, as I don't think the missus would have been too happy!'

He tells Dan that, when it comes to his career, it's important to forget about the money and the job – the one that will separate him from his friends, family and girlfriend for the next couple of months. 'Ask anyone on the street. You do a job, you want to be happy doing it. I've always said from day one, "If I did this job and I wasn't happy, I'd walk." I worked in a call centre. If I hadn't liked it, I would've walked. I wanted to do a job that I wanted to do.'

Later, away from the newspaper journalists, he thinks more about money, fame and happiness. 'I made that decision to do music because I wanted to do something that made me happy, and music gave me that something. It wasn't about money – it was never about money.'

Money helps, though.

'It doesn't make you happy... but it does make everything around you so much easier.'

—

It's an hour before show time. Olly's hair is being styled. On the table in his dressing room are his in-ear monitors – the headphones that allow him to hear his vocals and band over the screaming crowd. On the exterior of each monitor is a small photograph. It's a portrait of his nephew, Louie, the four-year-old son to his sister, Faye. 'I love him,' says Olly. 'He's so cute.'

He thinks about a time when he might have his own family. 'It's not in my thought process at the moment – it's not even close,' he says. 'I'm not thinking, *I'm ready to get married or have kids*. I dunno, it's not in my proximity right now.

'It's something that I eventually want to do but I'm not in that frame of mind. There's too much going on, too many exciting things are happening. I'm not in the right place to say, "OK guys, let's stop my career so I can have kids and family." I can't let this job go because it's so important to me. I'm gonna keep riding the wave.'

There's no time frame in place, but he doesn't want to be an old parent. 'Though I'm gonna try to enjoy my youth and what I've been given,' he says.

He never planned to get married, or settle down in his early twenties, the life that his parents wanted for him. 'Every life's different. I never wanted to be having kids when I was 20, 21 or 22. I wasn't that kinda guy. I wanted to be out and about, seeing the world, having fun; I wanted to settle down when I was in my late twenties. Now I've got past that and I'm in my early thirties, so at some point it'll happen, but not in the next couple of years. I've got too much going on.'

He thinks back to the time when his parents doubted the way his life was working out. 'Dad gave a great quote once when he said in an interview, "I wanted him to get a proper job, to have a proper family, earn good money... But what do we know? That's what we wanted for our son but he completely rewrote his own life... He did it his own way."'

—

Mark knocks on Olly's door. It's 8:30 pm: time to go. The band is assembling in the corridor outside – they're dressed in burgundy suits, black shoes, black shirts. Katie and Louise are running through vocal harmonies; there's talk of successful 'safety wees' – a last minute toilet stop-off before nearly two hours of performance. When Olly emerges in his stage outfit of black jacket with white band, grey shirt underneath, his energy levels are high; standing still seems to be a problem as everyone poses for press photographs. Walking as a group even brings its own sense of drama: Mike, Paul and Kenji break into the call-to-arms fanfare from the *Rocky* soundtrack as Olly shadow boxes his way to the backstage stairs.

Outside in the seats, the Motorpoint Arena's sell-out crowd is beginning to stir. Pharrell Williams's hit single 'Happy' pulses from the speakers; fans chant Olly's name. Behind the two-storey stage, the band gather as what looks like a small party breaks out. Kenji, Mike and Paul are now playing the Rebirth Brass Band's soulful hit, 'Feel Like Funkin' It Up', as used on the opening scenes to the HBO drama, *Treme*. Mark is geeing up the band, urging them to clap harder, to sing louder. This rousing walk-out anthem was his suggestion on a previous tour. 'It gets everyone pumped and ready to go,' he says. 'It's a ritual. It's our going-to-war chant.' The band claps in time as they close around Olly. They're singing – 'I feel like funkin' it up, feel like funkin' it up...'

Olly begins to yell. There are high fives and hugs as he stands in the middle of the group. 'OK, guys. Let's have an amazing show tonight,' he shouts over the building noise. 'Smile. Dance. Have a good time.'

Mark is counting them down. 'Thirty seconds, everyone. Thirty seconds...'

'I'm going to give you the same team talk that United's manager, Louis van Gaal gave to the boys before they spanked Liverpool,' says Olly.

Everyone leans in.

'We need to get out there and... *Unleash!*'

Mark hands him a mic. His band disappears up a flight of stairs that lead to the stage. Out front, the lights are killed. The backdrop masking his impressive stage construction falls to the floor, and a deafening roar ricochets around the Motorpoint Arena's cavernous walls. Olly is hyped now. The machine-gunning guitars of 'Misirlou' ping across the arena. Clenching his fists, he lands a one-two combination of jabs on Mark's bicep – 'Shit! I broke my wrist!' he laughs, shaking out the pain in his hand.

Mark gives him the thumbs up. Together they disappear under the performance area, heads down, towards his big entrance.

The man-lift propels him skywards. As Olly hits stage level, he springs up, pinning his arms by his side, his pose frozen. A spotlight frames his silhouette at the edge of the catwalk that stretches out into the crowd. There's a moment of confusion as the first ten rows, the fans positioned between him and the runway, fail to spot his arrival – he's behind them. Then the screaming starts. Olly stands still for a second or two, soaking up the adulation, the screams and the shouts. He nods approvingly, a hand cupped to his ear, just like in rehearsals.

'Did you miss me?' he sings.

The noise, the flashlights, a whirlpool of glowing mobile phones – it gives him all the confirmation he needs.

—

Olly wriggles his backside over the stage. He dances through 'Right Place Right Time', the backdrop a blitz of flickering lights; sweat drips off him as he orchestrates a tide of swaying arms during the chorus – 'Right here and now feels like forever. Never touch the ground when we're together. Right here and now feels like forever, forever, forever, forever...' John, Darren, Katie and Louise bolster his vocal with soaring harmonies.

He walks to the edge, reaching into the crowd. Hands stretch out to grab him.

'Welcome to the tour,' he says, waving to the back seats. 'It's a pleasure to be in your company this evening. And, of course, this is the first night!'

There's more cheering.

'So thank you so much for coming out tonight. I really, really, really, *really* appreciate it – I do.'

Olly smiles at the faces looking back at him from the front row – 'Now, I just want to get closer...'

He leans in, grabs a towel from the floor and quickly holds it against his crotch. He winks at the front row – 'Well, we all know what happened last time...'

—

The hits flash by in a rush. The swing of 'Why Do I Love You' has him strutting downstage, spinning, bouncing on the spot. The us-against-the-world lyricism of 'Never Been Better' is delivered in front of a bank of TV screens, each one orbiting *Tron*-style 3D graphics seemingly towards the audience. At the song's close, Olly drops to his knees, flanked by cannons of explosive pyrotechnics. He later encourages the crowd to sing the backing harmonies on 'Seasons' and they echo every note. This is when he feels the happiest: those moments when his fans buckle themselves in for a roller-coaster ride.

'You know what? I've got four albums!' he shouts triumphantly. '*Four!* Hands up if you bought all four...'

A sea of fists rush up from the crowd. 'It was so hard picking the songs to play to you,' he says.

He decides to tease everyone. 'So I'm gonna apologise... because I'm leaving.'

There are playful boos. He laughs.

'Of course I'm not gonna do that to you, darlings! But I'm gonna apologise because there are some songs you're not gonna hear.'

He begins to list them.'"Heart Skips a Beat" – gone. "Dance with Me Tonight" – gone. "Dear Darlin'" – gone.'

The crowd begins to yell.

'I said you were gonna be upset tonight!'

He quickly brings the mood around. 'I'm only joking! Blood, sweat and tears went into this set, so I hope you like it. Please. I beg you, *please*.'

He clasps his hands together. 'And if you do send me any horrible messages on Twitter, I will come to your house and I will do naughty, horrible things.'

A grin cuts across his face. 'It's not gonna be nice,' he warns, mock scolding the fans. 'I'm gonna get a bit Mr Grey on you.'

—

There are sombre moments, too. A nostalgic, stripped-back medley of older hits – 'Please Don't Let Me Go', 'Thinking Of Me', 'Busy' – is delivered from Sean's piano. When a steel walkway descends from the ceiling during 'Dance with Me Tonight', all blinking strip lights and industrial gangways, connecting him to an island stage at the back of the venue, he brings as intimate a vibe as anyone can to a 13,000 capacity arena. 'Let Me In', the ballad written with moddish singer-songwriter, Paul Weller, becomes a rousing, crowd singalong. Later, 'Dear Darlin'', a love letter penned by a heartbroken boyfriend to his departing lover, is soul-bruised: onstage he mentions his nan's death. His voice begins to tremble.

'I lost her three weeks ago,' he says. 'My best mate also lost his mum two years ago and this song was played at her funeral – it was one of her favourites. It took the song to a completely different place...'

He regains a little composure and draws breath. 'This song means so, so much to me, so if you're here with friends, or family, please give them a big hug from me – give that love out.' In the seats, everyone begins to cuddle.

—

There is a problem with his in-ear monitors. Olly can't hear the band properly. Between songs, he drops to his knees to question a sound technician positioned in the runway below him. For the briefest of moments his connection with the crowd has been cut. Only a joke can restore his momentum. 'Sorry,' he says, raising an apologetic hand to the audience. 'I just had to order a *Domino's*.'

—

'I am absolutely buzzing.'

Olly is standing in his pants, gulping down a bottle of water backstage, reliving the first show of the tour. He's pleased with the songs, the audience, the band. Every single moment worked, he thinks, apart from 'Did You Miss Me'. Apparently his voice had cracked a little in the opening verse. 'That was down

to the adrenaline, and the excitement. It doesn't bother me though, and I don't think the fans care either. They'd just seen me pop up from the floor...'

It was emotional, too.

'"Dear Darlin"'? Yeah, I know. I got really emotional. More than I thought I would, so I had to calm it down. I could have cried before I sang the song. As soon as I mentioned my best mate's mum, and I mentioned my nan, I don't know... For some reason, it was the room, the people, the vibe. I was totally lost. I didn't know what part of the song I was singing. I was thinking of my family, and my nan, and my mate. That's why it connects with me – it makes me think of the people that aren't in my life anymore.'

—

There's no more time for reflection. Olly's in the post-show high. When he runs into the band's dressing room, there's a loud cheer. He's still dressed in nothing but his grey Calvin Klein underpants.

OLLY ON THE RECORD: SETTLING DOWN

I've got the most amazing job in the world, performing every night and singing to crowds of thousands. But when I first decided that I wanted to be a singer, it seemed like a pipe dream to some people. When I told Mum and Dad that I was auditioning for *X Factor* in 2009 – my third stab at it – they were like, 'Are you sure that this is the right thing to do?'

I knew I had to have another shot. I said, 'Look, all you've got to worry about is this: am I paying you rent? Yeah. Then just worry about that. You're my parents, you want me to pay my way, I'm paying my way. Every month your money is coming in, it's on the table, so leave me to do what I've got to do. I know you want me to leave home. I know you want me to get married, I know you want me to have kids. I'll get there eventually, just let me do my thing. Let me take my own path.'

They did, they bit their tongues, and luckily it all worked out for me. But yeah, I want to have my own family in the future. I want to get married and settle down at some point. But I don't think I'm gonna get to that stage just yet. Most of the time, I live every day as it happens – I don't try to think too far ahead. Sure, sometimes I'll have to look ahead in my job. I have to consider when I'm next going to be touring, or when I might have to be in the studio for a couple of months to work on an album. But really, I live day by day, week by week.

The only time I'll take a break from all of this is when I have kids. And, even then, it'll all depend on the timing. In an ideal world I would take two years off work, while maybe doing a gig here and there, but that could all change if the demand for me to perform is high at the time. I might still be smashing tours. I might have an amazing tune that year, in which case I'll have to deal with those things as and when they happen. It's easy for me to say what I want now, but I know I can't always get that. It can all change in a heartbeat.

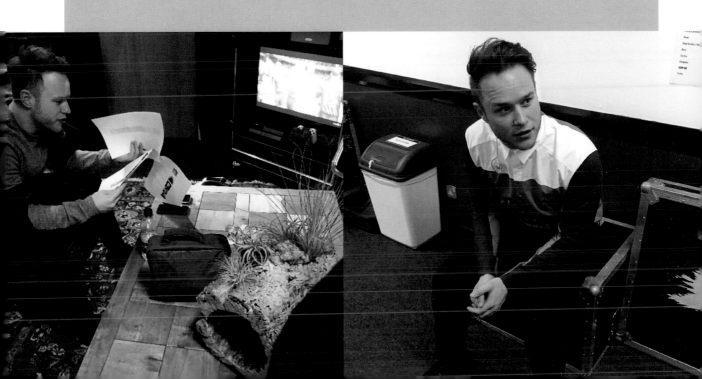

Chapter Six

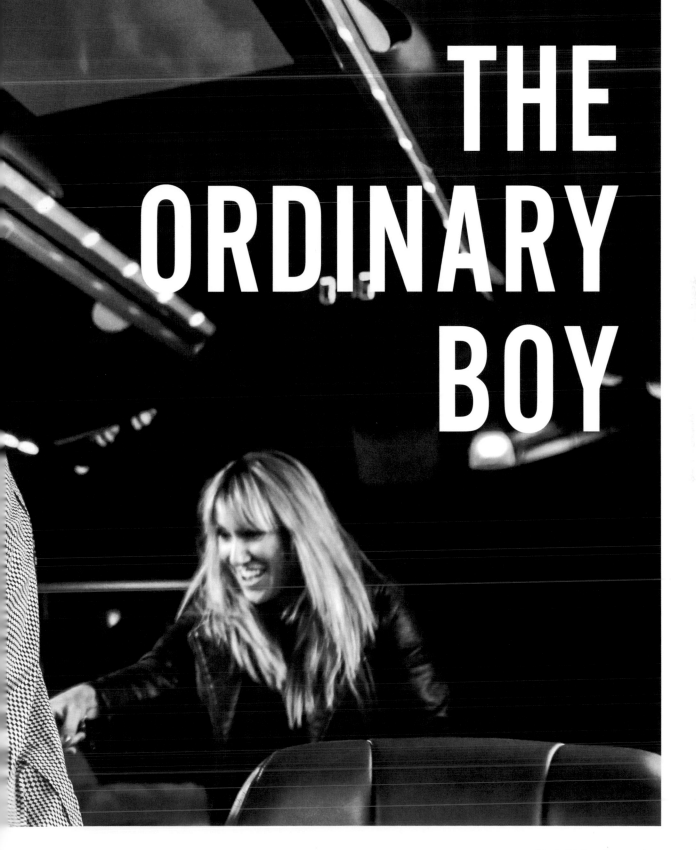

THE ORDINARY BOY

THE ORDINARY BOY

In Cardiff, his friends from Essex arrive for an Easter weekend party – the first of several gatherings on the tour. They begin daytime drinking on the train and arrive at the venue, another Motorpoint Arena, frazzled and rowdy. By the time his after-show celebrations have fizzled out in a city centre nightclub, one of them has thrown up in an ice bucket. The following morning, Olly's a little unhappy with their behaviour.

'I've had to tell them it was uncalled for,' he says. 'They were smashed before the gig had even started, and obviously this is a family show, so I was a little bit embarrassed.'

They've been given a warning, he says. 'I told them, "Look, if you're coming up to the gig, you're here to represent me, you're my mates."'

It was a case of some tough love. 'I had to tell them straight. They got the message, loud and clear.'

Olly reckons there won't be any hard feelings, though. The bonds are too tight. He's known most of these friends for ten years, and they've supported him through the ups and downs of his life. They've learned how to manage the fame together, which can be problematic at times, especially during a Saturday night out in Essex, when there's sometimes the issue of where to go and what to do; the clubs they can dance in without too much hassle, and the curry houses he can eat at unnoticed.

At first it was tough. 'Try explaining to your mates that you can't join them for a normal night out at the Romford Dogs because I'll probably get hassled out of it.' Other times, when they catch up for drinks, Olly says he forgets the

He's thinking about his friends again the next day. Not the lads that came to see him in Cardiff, but those who fell by the wayside as his fame increased. One time, shortly after his *X Factor* appearance, Olly bumped into an old mate on a shopping trip to Witham. Their brief exchange freaked him out a little.

'He was star-struck by me, which was so weird,' he says. 'We had a really good conversation and then he goes, "Oh my god, it's so strange talking to you... you're Olly Murs!" He couldn't believe that I'd got famous. Then he asked me for a picture, so I said to him, "Nah, you're my mate, what are you talking about?" I found it quite upsetting at the time. I was just Olly before he'd met me, and before I got famous...'

Then there were the friends that began criticising him behind his back. 'People who were supposed to be my best mates. They were saying that I'd changed, that I was an idiot. They said I was flash – all these things that I wasn't – and it really annoyed me. This one bloke was going around saying, "He's got money now, and a house, and he's on TV. He don't care about us no more." That wasn't the true story, but if people wanted to listen to that, well, that was their problem. But to anyone who knew me, I was never that person.'

There's a sigh. 'We all fall out with people at times... that's just the way it is.'

—

With three shows scheduled for the 3Arena in Dublin. Francesca has arrived to stay with him for a few days. It has been over a fortnight since Olly last saw her and he's looking forward to their alone time; just two of them together, away from the madness of the tour. A crowd gathers around Olly as he exits The InterContinental. The hotel has been chosen because of its distance from the city centre. Mark likes to keep his destinations secret, to hold the fans away for as long as possible, but they often find out after a day or two, usually via a dedicated process of trial and error. When somebody finally discovers the right venue – often through a series of sneaky phone calls to the reception desk, or by some snooping around a forecourt where Olly's people carrier can be spotted – the info is pinged across Twitter and Facebook.

In the car park, there's some pushing for his autograph. A few fans want to chat. Olly figures he has a little time to spare, so he stops to say hello. Then a disgruntled fan – a man in his mid-twenties – approaches the group. He's waving a diva-ish finger in Olly's direction. Apparently he used the The InterContinental's side entrance last night rather than greeting the kids waiting for him by the main door.

'Even Beyoncé came through and said hello after her shows,' says the fan, snootily. 'Why can't you?'

Olly begins to apologise. 'I was tired last night mate, I'm so sorry...'

'I could drop you...' says the fan, clicking his fingers dramatically, 'like that.'

Mark butts in, ushering everyone away, 'Or we could always drop you,' he laughs. 'Come on, Oll.'

He gets into the people carrier, sliding the door shut behind him. Live commentary of the Grand National is playing on the radio and Mark has a bet on; his horse is well-placed in the leading pack.

'The thing with the National is that sometimes the horse wakes up, feels a bit knackered and can't be arsed,' says Olly. 'A bit like me today.'

—

There's some frantic patting of pockets. Francesca has forgotten her tour laminate, the Access All Areas pass that allows anyone in Olly's crew to wander backstage unchallenged by security. Olly starts laughing.

'It's still a one strike and you're out policy, isn't it Mark?'

'Oh, yes,' confirms Mark, sternly. He's known as a stickler for tour security.

Members of his crew are occasionally yelled at for not following the right procedures.

'Use mine, babe,' says Olly. 'It's not like they won't let me in, is it?' Then he remembers. 'Oh yeah, except for that time when I was doing a summer show a couple of years back – Pixie Lott was supporting – where Mark?'

'Wales?' says Mark.

'No, it was Doncaster. We got there really early, so we had time to relax and do nothing. Mark was in meetings, so I thought, *Sod it, I'll have a little walk around, to see where everything is.* I went to go into the bar and somehow walked out of the backstage area instead. When I tried to get back in, this security guy went, "Excuse me sir, where's your pass?"

'I said, "What? Sorry mate, I haven't got it on me."

'"I can't let you back in then…" he goes.

'I said, "Don't be silly, this is my gig, I'm performing. I'm the guy on the badge." He was having none of it, though.

'Then the promoter came round and sorted it out. I went straight up to Mark…'

For the next part of the story he adopts a whiney voice. 'I said, "Mark! That guy out there wouldn't let me in because I didn't have my pass." Mark looked furious. He says, "Where is he?" So he goes storming off, looking for the geezer…'

Mark interjects. 'And when I got there, I shook his hand and said, "Well done on doing your job, mate. If Olly hasn't got the right pass, he can't come in."'

—

With a temporary pass located for Francesca, Olly settles into the band's dressing room. Mellissa is styling his hair. He's taken his top off for the trim. Between snips he tenses his biceps and sings to his reflection in the mirror.

Francesca sighs. 'This is what I get every morning,' she says. 'He's always showing off.'

Mellissa stands back to check the quiff. She ruffles his hair at the sides. Olly begins to fidget.

'We're done, yeah?'

She nods.

He rises from his chair. 'Sweet!' he declares loudly. 'Sweet as a nut bag!'

He stretches out on the sofa. The room clears. His only duty between now and show time is to sign a box of VIP programmes for a list of invited guests.

This is now a daily routine, and he's familiar with the workload, though he admits to being a little edgier than usual tonight. It's Francesca's arrival. With his girlfriend around, he wants the show to be perfect.

'I wanna impress her,' he says. 'I'm a bit nervous, but it's an excitable nervousness. I want to make sure that everything's bang on tonight.'

There have been other concerns since Francesca's arrival on the scene three years ago. It doesn't surround the two of them, or their relationship. Instead Olly's high-profile lifestyle, and the complications that come with it, can prove problematic sometimes. At first, he kept their relationship a secret from journalists because he wanted to protect their privacy. He was also worried about how female fans might react to the announcement of a new girlfriend.

'I didn't want it to be a public relationship,' he says. 'Yeah, it's public to my friends and family, which every relationship is, but why should my relationship be any different because I'm a singer in the industry? A pop star? Why should my relationship be splattered across the papers every week, or across magazines?

'Also Francesca's not famous. She's not in this job, so I wanted her to keep her life as well. We'd only been with each other nine months when it was announced. But say we were in the papers every day, and it had changed her life – and it was affecting her life badly – we might not be where we are now. It might have affected us too much. But because I've kept my work separate from us, we're able to have a normal relationship. We're able to have normal lives.'

And what is normality for you two?

'After shows, I'll get in the car and go home. We'll watch movies, lounge around and eat dinner, like normal couples do. It's not like we can't go out at all – it's just that we might see a movie when it's quiet, or we'll book a restaurant for a Monday or a Tuesday, rather than Saturday night when loads of people are going to be around.'

It's not like his fame is a new thing to Francesca. 'She knew what my life was like before we met up,' he says. Still, the public reveal of their coupling, when it arrived, was annoying. 'Some stupid idiots took pictures of us at a wedding. That was really frustrating.' But so far, he says, the press has left them alone. He's

pleased about that. He'd like for the two of them to live their lives together, not through the public eye. It's important to him that Francesca remains her own person – 'Not that girl dating Olly Murs.'

—

Olly and Francesca are both aware of his position as a pop star, where as much emphasis is placed on sex appeal as his voice. Dealing with teenage crushes can be a delicate process.

'A lot of my fans are girls,' he says. 'So it can cause problems, obviously. Sometimes I'll ask Francesca to stay in the people carrier when a crowd comes around. From her perspective, she's thinking, "Why am I a secret? Why are you putting me in a car?" And I say, "You can come and stand with me if you want." But if someone comes up and asks for a picture and says, "Olly I really fancy you, you should dump your girlfriend. You should get rid of her and go out with me …" It's not nice.

'And the fans sometimes struggle to realise that I can't stop to talk every time. Then again, these fans have invested time in me since day one. They've met me every day, they've spent money to see me, and for the sake of 20 minutes, I don't see a problem in chatting with them. I've never had a problem with it. It's just that some days we're busy. Some days we can't hang around. It's just one of them things.'

Wouldn't it be easier for you to hide away altogether?

'You have to appreciate them. I've never shied away. I've never avoided the fans – only when there's been a problem with safety, or time. Like, if people are saying, "Olly it isn't safe, we have to go," then that's what we have to do. Leona Lewis was doing a book signing once and a fan slapped her in the face. I'm an adult, I'm a man, I can look after myself, but there's a level of security I need.

'But if it's cool, I'll say hello. Even if I've had a bad day, or if I'm in a bad mood, I'll always stop to say thank you for the amazing support if I can. I'd have nothing without them.'

—

There are always gifts. The weirdest present a fan has ever given Olly was a three-piece suit from Ben Sherman. 'Fitted, exactly to my size,' he says. 'I couldn't believe it.' More recently a bobble hat with his portrait stuck to the wool was thrust into his hands. Most of the time, though, he's presented with ceramic mugs. The photograph of his giving fan is often printed on the front. 'They want me to have a cuppa tea in the morning and think of them, I guess.'

—

In every city there is local press to do, radio interviews aimed at hyping the show. Everyone tries to catch him out on the *X Factor* appointment. It's a game of cat and mouse that usually runs along these lines:

Interviewer: 'So, congrats on getting the *X Factor* job, Olly! You must be excited...'

He shrugs them off every time. There are comments about the headlines being 'just rumours', speculation, how he doesn't want the position unless Caroline Flack is involved. 'They all want me to slip up,' he says.

In reality, his appointment is all but agreed. Simon Cowell has been calling Olly's mobile, 'putting the pressure on', urging him to sign the contract so his revamped line-up can be announced to fans of the show. 'But at the end of the day, *X Factor* isn't about Caroline and me,' says Olly. 'The show is about the judges and the contestants. As long as we get a great bunch of contestants this year, we'll be there to support them. I'm excited about it.'

Behind the scenes, there are some small concerns being voiced by one or two of his management team regarding the new job. The main worry is that Olly's TV role might quickly distract the public from his position as one of the biggest solo artists the show has ever produced. Whenever this issue is mentioned, he starts repeating those stats: four albums since his emergence in 2009, three of them number ones. He's proved himself in the charts, he says. Now he's after a fresh challenge.

'I think I need *something*,' he says before warming up in his dressing room. 'Another focus, something to get my teeth into. Music is great, I love songwriting and I love touring, and I love all of this, but I miss TV, and this has given me a perk. I'm excited. I've got a bit of a buzz in my stomach. I need to challenge myself. Look, *X Factor* might be the best thing I do, it might be the worst thing. Who knows?'

And there's no guarantees about how long your music career might go on for.

'Yeah, exactly. I might get fat and bald and then it's over.'

—

Dublin is the first standing show of the tour. A thousand or so fans move on the dance floor in front of him, thousands of packed seats rise up behind, but there's one stony face in the crowd: a man with his girlfriend, who by bad luck happens to be standing in the front row. At first, he refuses to dance, despite his partner's enthusiastic pleading. She tugs his shirt and playfully nudges him on the arm. Later, she jabs an elbow angrily into his ribs. Still there's no response. He stands at the barrier for the entire show, his arms folded defiantly. By the end of the evening, his girlfriend looks just as miserable. If body language is a window into this relationship, it's unlikely they're still together.

Olly spots the arguing. After the show, he seems miffed.

'I really wanted to pull that geezer out of the crowd,' he says as he's driven away from the 3Arena. 'Did you see him? That guy in the front row? He would not have a good time. At one point I was gonna say to him, "Excuse me mate... Can we get the cameras on this guy? You didn't wanna come here tonight, did you? You've basically missed a really good stag do... Or your best mate's birthday, or something, because you *really* don't want to be here."'

Sarah later explains how Olly often likes to locate an unmoving spectator in the crowd, usually a newspaper or magazine critic in the guest seats, before directing his energy their way until they relent, by nodding appreciatively at least.

'He just won't have people not enjoying themselves,' she says.

OLLY ON THE RECORD: FRIENDSHIP

My friends are so important to me – they help me to lead a relatively normal life when I'm at home. If I'm not on tour, or away working, we'll often get together for dinner; sometimes we'll end up in a nightclub somewhere in Essex. Normally I'll hear of something special going on, or someone will tip us off about a cool event, but whatever we've got planned I can't wait to catch up with the guys when I get home.

It can be tricky though. There have been times when I've had to change plans because I've been told that loads of fans are likely to be around. Those situations can sometimes become quite awkward. My mates end up turning into photographers all night, and I get frustrated because I can't have a good laugh without getting hassled by strangers. That's when I'll say, 'Nah lads, let's do something different.' On occasions it's been easier just to get the boys around to my house for a few beers and a game of FIFA, though there have been occasions where I've been able to treat everybody by getting us VIP tickets to a movie premiere or football match.

I trust my mates, though, and I don't keep anything back from them. But I would never tell them what I earned, or what I got paid for a gig. I'd never tell them how much I'd paid for a car. I like to keep anything to do with money to myself. That's been my rule since I was 13 years old. My granddad once said to me, 'Listen Olly, what you earn is what you earn – no one should know that information. *No one*.' That's always stuck with me. So I'm very conscious of that. If I say, 'Bought myself a new car today,' someone will ask, 'How much did that set you back?'

I'll say, 'Oh, too much – know what I mean?'

I know there's a lot of people that would say, 'It cost me this much money,' or, 'I've just spent this amount on a new house.' But when I hear that kind of thing, I always think, 'Alright mate, chill out.' That's not the type of person I am.

Over the years, I've realised that this industry is full of acquaintances rather than mates. There are people I work with that are friends, yeah. But the rest are acquaintances. They're people that I really respect. I can have a laugh with them, and work with them, but they're not people I'll hang out with at home. The mates that I'll go on couples' dinners with; the people I meet for lunch, and play football with; the friends I go clubbing with, or go on holiday with? They're proper mates.

I think the friends I've got around me now are friends I'll have for the rest of my life. They understand me. They understand my lifestyle and the difficulties that come with it; they keep me grounded. I have that much love and respect for them that I can't see it being ruined.

OLLY ON THE SETLIST

So much hard work and thought went into planning the setlist for 2015's *Never Been Better* tour. When you have four albums to choose from, deciding what songs to leave out can be tricky because I knew it meant that some fans might not get to hear their favourite tracks live. Then there was the actual order to think about – I wanted to take people on a journey with my singles and album cuts, while performing in an exciting show. It took a while to get it all in place. Hopefully my choices delivered in a big way...

1. DID YOU MISS ME

There's no bigger buzz than being onstage, but when you're an artist and you've been out of the limelight for a little while, like I had before the release of *Never Been Better*, it's easy to develop little insecurities. I'd see other artists coming out and doing really well. I watched people having big records and successes, number one albums and massive singles. A lot of my fans on Facebook and Twitter were supporting new female artists, or up-and-coming boy bands. I figured it would be easy for people to jump ship, especially when someone they'd previously been following hadn't done anything new for a while – like me.

When it came to making the latest album, I had this idea of writing a song for the fans with the lyrics: 'What you've been doing now that since I've been away? Have you been good? Have you been bad? Did you behave? It's alright...' It was basically my way of telling the fans that I was back, that I wanted to take them into my life again. When it came to planning the tour, it seemed like the perfect opening song.

2. RIGHT PLACE RIGHT TIME

I've always believed in the saying, 'you've gotta be in the right place at the right time', and this song carries that same sentiment. It's weird because when it was first written, the idea behind the words focused on that buzz you sometimes experience when encountering someone new, exciting; when you get that feeling of meeting a special person in the right place at the right time. That's always an incredible moment. It can make you stop and think... *Wow!*

Songs can change meaning as they get older, though. These days, I also feel like the song has a lot to say about my work. Everything fell into place during the 2015 UK tour, what with the album, the shows and my getting a presenter's role on *X Factor*.

But it's been like that throughout my whole career. The first three or four years were amazing. Things were happening, everything I touched seemed to pan out really well – it was all taking shape. It didn't feel out of control (though there were a couple of hard moments), but it was definitely a crazy ride. Big offers were coming in, and there were TV shows, albums, singles and tours. I performed with the likes of Robbie Williams and One Direction. It was crazy. And a lot of it was about timing.

3. WHY DO I LOVE YOU

When certain songs come on in the set, I can feel the energy within the crowd building, getting bigger. This is one of those moments. I started planning the show at the end of 2014 and I wanted the opening to be a powerful introduction because, for me, it's such a huge feeling to be standing on that stage, in front of 15,000 fans, and performing my hits. But I didn't want to lose the crowd after the first two songs by playing a ballad. I wanted to keep the tempo high, and this song worked perfectly.

It's funny, when we first put 'Why Do I Love You' together the lyrics were quite downbeat. It's about a girl – the kind you meet who seems great on the surface. You fall in love with her, but then she turns into an absolute nightmare. You're left thinking, why did I bother? That mood changed when we got into the studio. The producers put a Rudimental-style, dubstep beat on it, and suddenly, 'Why Do I Love You' sounded so cool – I've always loved it when an emotional song can make people dance. After the 'one-two' jab of the opening songs, it kept the tempo of my live show at a high level.

4. HEY YOU BEAUTIFUL

I love singing the lyrics to 'Hey You Beautiful'. They're cheeky, with a really flirtatious vibe, and the song always gets people moving in their seats because it's got a nice funkiness to it.

The funny thing about this one is that it was originally called 'Sex in Your Eyes', which was a line in the lyrics: 'Whoa-oh, I know it, Whoa-oh, you got it, Whoa-oh, sex is in your eyes.' In the end, we thought a title like that might be considered too naughty, so we changed it at the last minute.

'Hey You Beautiful' is a story about meeting a gorgeous girl; I'm flirting, the pair of us are having a great night. Sometimes you can meet a person and sense an immediate chemistry. You know right then that whatever happens between you – and it might be a one off, or it could last a couple of months – there's going to be a real passion; it's going to be a physical relationship rather than a proper one.

5. HAND ON HEART

When I came to recording this for *Right Place Right Time* in 2012, it was a song that had already been half-done by the songwriters, Ben Kohn, Tom Barnes, Wayne Hector, Iain James and Peter Kelleher, plus the production team, TMS. I loved the hook straightaway and it's become a great singalong live – while playing it, I'd often ask the fans to put their hands somewhere *naughtier*. At the end of the song, during the last chorus, I'd walk to the edge of the stage, stick my backside out and sing, 'Put your hand on my...' I'd leave the final word to their imaginations! I love interacting with a crowd.

I've done four tours now, so I know the kind of jokes my audiences enjoy. During the intro to 'Hand on Heart' I'd even announce, 'Birmingham! (Or wherever we were that night.) Do you take me, Olly Murs, to be your

lawful, wedded husband? And now... we're married!' I've always been like that, though. When I did my first tour, it was stripped back – just me with the band, a mic and some songs – and I'd always have plenty of banter with the fans, but no one told me what to say onstage, no one on my team told me what to talk about. I just went out there and did it.

6. NEVER BEEN BETTER

When we began rehearsals in February, I loved how this song sounded. With my band behind me, it felt huge, a real moment. After 'Hand on Heart', we planned it so I could run offstage to change my shirt, because, believe me, it would get bloody hot up there. I'd towel down and dry off; Mellissa would restyle my hair. I'd be back onstage within a minute, but I wanted to begin the next part of the show with a real bang. Once I'd heard 'Never Been Better' being played in our studio in SW19, I knew it was the perfect comeback.

I think a lot about my set and what order the songs are played in. A few other people from management have had their say on what songs they think should go where, but I've often rejigged it around to the point where I thought the set was right. I know that when it comes to the songs, and what I'm doing onstage, that's my job. That's what I do.

This song is a big moment in the show. When it was written, I guess this was a way of responding to my critics. It was the chance for me to say, 'Regardless of what people say or think about me, where I've come from 'till now, I've never been better. Life's good.' That's exactly how I feel now. Am I happy in what I'm doing? Yes. Am I having a great time? Yes. And am I loving my life? Yes – *brilliant*. Well, in which case, I've never been better.

I wanted to get some things off my chest with this one, too. A few people have said that I'm still chasing Robbie Williams's crown, which is annoying. Then there were the critics that slammed me when I first started out as an artist. I deal with that stuff during one of the verses when I sing, 'The world can't knock me down, cos I won't take defeat… I'm still around, look who's winning now.'

Obviously I lost the *X Factor* final when I finished as runner up in 2009, and people were saying that I was crap; they thought that I wasn't any good. There were doubters. That lyric says, 'Sod you, I'm winning now.' I know that's an arrogant thing to say in a song, but why not? I'm fighting my corner.

But 'Never Been Better' is also a rallying cry for anyone that might be feeling a bit down in life; for people who need a bit of a pick-me-up. I know what that's like because I've been there. When I was working in a call centre, back in the days before *X Factor*, I wasn't enjoying myself. Some of my fans might be in a similar place themselves now, and I know a lot of people out there have taken inspiration from this song. They get a more positive spin on things after hearing it, and 'Never Been Better' is one of those tracks that I'm really proud of. It's personal to me. It's a song about appreciating what you already have in life.

I remember I did a five-day trek in Kenya for Comic Relief in 2011. It was an amazing experience, and I'll never forget it. But I remember that one day we went into this house in the middle of nowhere. We were there to help a woman who had trachoma, which is a contagious bacterial condition that affects the eyes. When we got to her place, my feeling was that we had no right to be there. Yeah, we had turned up to help, but it was as if we were looking at her and saying, 'Ahhh, I feel sorry for you. You're living in a hut in the middle of the desert and you haven't got what we've got.'

But then I thought, *Nah, I'm looking at this the wrong way. She's happy, her family's happy. They're loving their lives.* It's easy to get caught up in comparing your situation to others – for good and for bad. Sometimes it helps to think about what you have in *your* life and to be grateful for it: family, health, work – whatever makes you happy. 'Never Been Better' takes that idea on, too.

7. SEASONS

This was another song that involved the crowd. I wanted to make sure that I had plenty of chat with them on this tour, so whenever I introduced 'Seasons', I got them to 'whoop' the high-pitched backing vocals that run through the track. I even got the song rearranged in rehearsals so every arena could get a chance to sing it without me. The fans nailed it every night.

For me, when I perform, I want an audience to feel like they're a big part of the show. It's not really about putting loads of jokes and funny moments in-between the songs. It's about them seeing my personality, and connecting, because what you see is what you get with me onstage. It's who I am. I want them to really feel that they've been involved when they walk away from one of my gigs.

'Seasons' is basically a story about a relationship where the girl doesn't trust her other half. She keeps reading and hearing stories about her boyfriend and they're upsetting. I've been lucky. I've not really experienced that situation myself. Yeah, there's been the occasional story, some gossip, silly things in the papers, but it's never been that bad. I remember when Francesca and me first got together, there were a few articles flying around where girls were discussed. That happened because our relationship was fresh at the time. The papers thought that I was still single and so there'd be little write-ups which said, 'Oh, Olly likes these kind of girls.' Or, 'So and so is his type.' Because the papers know I've got a girlfriend now, things have changed. They don't run those stories anymore.

8. PIANO MEDLEY: THINKING OF ME / BUSY / PLEASE DON'T LET ME GO

I've always had a medley section in my live shows because I like to slow the pace down a bit in the middle of a gig. In the past I've used an acoustic guitar; last time around I had a guitar and a piano. But this year I wanted it to be slick, classy, so I decided on just the piano, which was played by my musical director Sean. John, Darren, Louise and Katie delivered all the backing vocals for stripped-back takes on three of my earliest hits.

'Please Don't Let Me Go', 'Thinking Of Me' and 'Busy' were songs from my first album that I knew the fans loved, but I wanted to present them in a different way. I thought a piano medley, which showed off my voice and my amazing backing singers, worked great in the end. It took the show to a different place. The piano acoustics, the voices, those harmonies: it all helped to create a beautiful mood.

It also meant the fans could reminisce on my earlier hits. But to be honest, I wasn't sure if the medley would work when we planned it out, even in rehearsals. That changed from the first show in Sheffield. I knew we had got it right because the crowd sang along to every word.

9. HOPE YOU GOT WHAT YOU CAME FOR

This song had two meanings when I recorded it for *Never Been Better*. The first hook was for the fans – just like 'Right Place Right Time' and 'Did You Miss Me' I was already thinking ahead to the tour, and I'm saying, 'I hope you got what you came for.' I wanted to know that they were having a good time, which is why there are a few references to performance and being a showman buried in the lyrics – 'You and I, you and I, always the same thing, every time, every time, you come around, tell me now, tell me now, why are you leaving, is it time, is it time, to take a bow?'

When I'm in the studio writing I'm often trying to create lyrics that the fans can really connect to when I'm performing for them. I'm asking them a question here, but I suppose it shows more of the insecurities that I have as an artist, like on 'Did You Miss Me' In the same way that I hoped the fans had thought about me while I'd been writing and recording in a studio somewhere, I also wanted to know that they'd enjoyed themselves during the show.

The original idea for the song was a lot darker than that, though. When it started out, it was a story about feeling used by somebody. Sometimes there can be situations where a person comes into your life and they take you for their own means. That's when you think, *Well, I hope you got what you came for. You just seemed to use me. You came into my life, took whatever it was that you wanted, and then you went again.*

I've been in that situation before and it's not a nice place to be. And I've probably also been the person doing it to someone else as well.

10. HEART SKIPS A BEAT

The moment when my show goes, *boom*! 'Heart Skips a Beat' is one of those songs that always gets a big reaction. It's a track that's been a huge hit for me and it's been great to play for the past three or four years. It's got a big personality.

When we first started playing this on the *Never Been Better* tour, it had a different groove. It was funkier. We'd used that version on the Radio One Live Lounge sessions and it had worked so well that I thought it would be great to play it on the tour in that same style. But when it came to our first night in Sheffield, the crowd didn't go for it. That was a shame, because I really loved the version we'd worked out. I guess it was a lesson, though. Sometimes there are songs that you can't change because so many people love them for what they are.

'Heart Skips a Beat' means a lot to me because it was the first number one from my second album, *In Case You Didn't Know*. At that point in my career, I was in a similar position to where I found myself during the 2015 tour, because I'd just been given the *Xtra Factor* job. Life was really busy, but back then I wasn't experienced. I became really conscious of whether people were going to buy my tunes because I'd just become a TV presenter. I felt really unsure of what was going to happen to my music. Was I still going be successful? Were the fans going to like it?

People told me that you couldn't do both – music and TV – but we proved them wrong with 'Heart Skips a Beat'. Despite being on TV, it was still massively successful in the charts, and when it got to number one it was a huge deal for me and a massive weight off my shoulders. Listen, I know that there will always be people who are going be judgmental. There will always be people who will criticise me, as well as people who will always be positive. But I have to get used to that because I'm a musician, I'm an artist, and I want people to still see me as that.

11. UP FT. ELLA EYRE

This was written in 2013, so I'd had it for a while before it finally got a release date the following year. The only question was, 'Who do we get to perform the duet?' We went around the houses and our eventual choice, Demi Lovato, was a singer I really liked. Her voice is amazing and we had chemistry in terms of sound. I also knew that she had been an *X Factor* judge, so we had a lot in common.

When we made it happen it sounded amazing, but the frustrating thing about doing a song with a brilliant artist like her, especially a duet, is that I can't really sing that song live without having someone else alongside me, a performer who's just as good. It was always going to be hard to find someone who sang as well as Demi.

Luckily, on the tour we had Ella Eyre as my support act. She was keen on singing 'Up', and once we'd started working on it, she sounded amazing. Ella's a huge talent. We first played it together on the Radio One Live Lounge sessions, which worked out great. Later, during rehearsals, she came in for an hour to work with me on the song. Right then, I knew she would smash it every night.

12. DANCE WITH ME TONIGHT

This is my biggest song, regardless. Forget about 'Troublemaker', 'Heart Skips a Beat', or 'Dear Darlin'': 'Dance with Me Tonight' was an instant hit. I knew when I wrote it that it was going to be massive, and whenever I play

it now it's such a crowd pleaser that I could end every show with it. I could probably start the gig with it, too. Wherever I go, it gets a huge reaction. Everyone who comes to a show of mine loves this single.

On the *Never Been Better* tour, a walkway came down from the ceiling and connected the main stage to another platform at the back of the arena. The idea was for me to perform a song from above the crowd as I danced over. I wanted to do something dramatic, and this song ticked all the boxes. It was brilliant looking down and seeing all the fans going crazy beneath me.

13. LET ME IN

What was great about 'Let Me In' was that I got to write it with Paul Weller. I'd loved him since I was a kid. I was a fan of his bands The Jam and The Style Council, and his solo stuff as well, so to go into the studio and write a song with him was a big moment for me.

I remember when I first met him, we were at a gig. Paolo Nutini was performing; I had got my photo taken with him and we ended up chatting. He said, 'I'll send you a song,' and a little while later he sent me over 'Let Me In'. I loved it but I thought it was very Paul Weller in style at first, and I wanted to put my own stamp on it, so I said, 'Can I do some writing on it, too?' He was up for it, and six weeks later I was in the studio working with him.

Performing it on tour was fun. I did this and 'Dear Darlin'' from the smaller, second stage at the back of the arena. At this point in the show, my voice became the focus, and the audience would often hold up their mobile phones as I sang. Sometimes, the whole crowd would light up while it was being played.

14. DEAR DARLIN'

The meaning in 'Dear Darlin'' has also changed over the years. When it was first recorded, the guy I was writing it with had wanted to sketch out a letter to his girlfriend in a song. The lyrics were his way of penning a note of love and affection.

Now the meaning's completely different. Two years ago, one of my best mates lost his mum and 'Dear Darlin'' was played at her funeral because it was her favourite song. It was a really sad moment for all of us, so these days the lyrics make me think of the people we lose in our lives, the ones we love the most.

For the tour, I wanted to strip the song back, so it was just my voice, backed by a piano. I figured it would be more emotive that way, and every time I've sung it recently, I've felt like I had to do it justice. I wanted to perform it with a real passion, so I'd think of my mate's mum, and my nan, and the other loved ones that I've lost in my life. I honestly think I'll do that for as long as I'm singing it because 'Dear Darlin'' means more to me today than it did when I recorded it.

15. FUNK MEDLEY

After those two slower songs, I wanted to get a party mood going. I've always done medleys in my show and I'm very proud of them. Before we got on the road, I had a real battle with myself over what the next thing should be. We'd already done a Stevie Wonder medley, and a James Brown one. Later, there was a rock jam where I covered the likes of The Clash and Madness. Then we did an Earth, Wind & Fire mash-up on the Robbie tour.

I decided that I wanted to keep that disco element because it had felt massive. I thought, *Right let's doing something fresh.* And with a funk medley we created a really good tempo. It took a lot of work, though. Loads of thought went into the mix – we had Chic's 'Le Freak' and 'Working Day and Night' by Michael Jackson; 'Play That Funky Music', which was originally recorded by Wild Cherry, and 'Rapper's Delight' by The Sugarhill Gang. We ended the section on 'Uptown Funk' by Mark Ronson, one of the biggest songs of 2014. After the first night, we knew it was amazing.

It lasted eight minutes and, whenever we played it, I wanted the crowd to party like it was a Saturday night. I'd tell them to forget about work or going to school because I wanted them to go crazy. The reaction was up there with all the other medleys we'd done in the past. My band rocked it every time.

16. BEAUTIFUL TO ME

I wrote this with my girlfriend in mind, but it's more about the concept of being in a relationship where your partner feels a little bit insecure, or left out. That's when they have to be told that they're amazing. The song is basically me saying, 'I don't care what happens outside of this – of us – it's about what happens with the two of us.'

I love the spirit of it, and the reaction to it on the tour was great. Although it's a new song, I think it's become about the fans too, because they're also beautiful to me. I really appreciate the fact that they're around all the time, supporting me, wherever I'm playing.

17. TROUBLEMAKER

Though people will probably know me from 'Dance with Me Tonight', in terms of sales this has been my biggest hit to date. I've sold over 2 million copies of 'Troublemaker' around the world, which has been amazing. It seemed fitting to end the show with it, before the encore, though I could have played it right at the very end, because it's that big.

Once it was recorded and out there, I remember hearing it for the first time on the radio. I was in New York. It was three o'clock in the afternoon, and we were driving around, when it suddenly came on, unannounced. I was there thinking, *Wow, I'm in New York and one of my songs is playing – that's ridiculous.*

Everything about that song was great to me, even the title. Sometimes singles have everything. The song is saying to someone, 'You're just a troublemaker.' It's cheeky and I loved pointing out faces in the crowd as I went through the chorus.

ENCORE
18. NOTHING WITHOUT YOU

A co-writer already had 'Nothing Without You' mapped out when it first came to me. I really liked the saying, 'There's no we without you' in a relationship, and so the lyrics became about a special person in my life. In the song I was letting that person know I was nothing without them; that the times I'd spent with them had been fantastic. I was telling them, 'You make me.'

Later, when I was in the rehearsal studios for this tour, I kept getting an overwhelming feeling every time I ran through the words. It was as if I was singing to every fan in the audience. I guess I'd experienced that because I knew I'd be nothing without them. Eventually, I figured it would be great to play this near the close of the show, where I could thank everybody by going: 'London, Liverpool, Sheffield, Manchester, Dublin... *wherever*: I'm nothing without you guys and all your support.'

I really hope they get that in the song, and the performance, because I'm always trying to get that feeling across. They're the best fans around.

19. WRAPPED UP

A few people in my team were surprised when I put 'Wrapped Up' at the finale of the show, but I knew it was a great ending because I understand my fans so well. I know what they like, and what they expect from my gigs. I've been

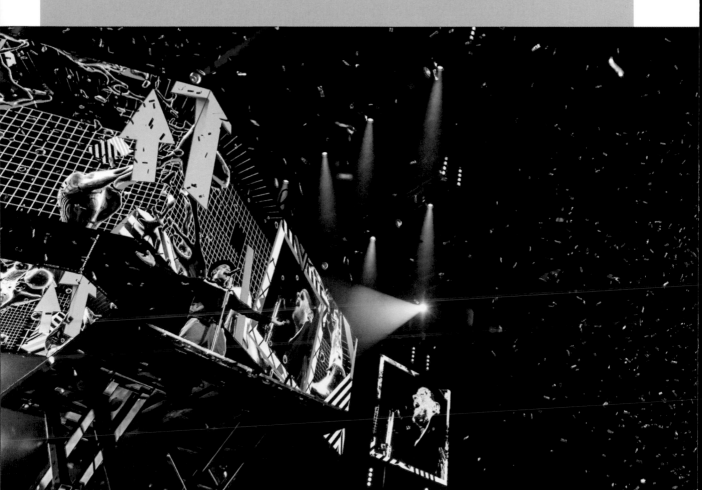

doing this for a long time and I get that this song is an all-round, feel-good disco tune that they're really into.

Whenever this came on at the end of every night, the crowd started bouncing because it's got that old-school club sound. Everyone buzzed off it and they left the venue on a massive high, like they wanted to go out dancing at the end of the night in some nearby club.

It looked good, too. At the close of the show a scissor lift rose out of the ground and took me about 15 feet up in the air, so I could look down on the crowd; loads of confetti fired out over the arena. It was crazy, but let me tell you, that lift was *wobbly*. I got used to it at the end, but, wow, it could be scary up there.

What I really loved about 'Wrapped Up' was that I could see people leaving halfway through the song. Normally that can be disheartening as a performer, but during the encore I'd watch as people danced their way out of the venue to get a head start on the journey home. They were waving back at me. It was as if I'd finished off a great night for them, and that felt pretty special.

Chapter Seven

'DO ENJOY YOUR STAY, MR CROW'

'DO ENJOY YOUR STAY, MR CROW'

Backstage at the SSE Hydro Arena in Glasgow, Olly is suffering from an episode of paranoia, the kind familiar to most celebrities of his stature. It starts with an email from his mum. There's some worrying news.

'She reckons a journalist has been asking about me at home,' he says. His brow furrows as he scrolls through the message. Apparently, a reporter has been making house calls, knocking at his parents' front door. His sister, Faye, experienced a similar intrusion shortly afterwards. Polite interview requests were made, 'for some background info on Olly', but the reporter's apparent reluctance to explain her angle (there was no mention of the paper's name, either) has everyone spooked. Olly scans his phone for more details.

'It doesn't bother me. It's more...'

He begins to lose his cool a little.

'Why would the papers be doing that?' he says, sighing. 'Why would someone be knocking at my mum and dad's door? Why would someone be knocking on my sister's door? That's not cool. And it's not professional. It's not clever. It infuriates me a little bit. *That's not cool.* You don't go hassling my mum and dad. Or my sister...'

He says it again, 'That's *not* cool.' He's wound up.

Five years into his career, Olly understands the game; interview requests aren't uncommon in his position, especially now, with the speculation regarding his future role at *X Factor*, but there's usually a well-followed procedure to complete before meetings and photoshoots can take place. As with most celebrities, media proposals are run through a publicist, in Olly's case, the office of Barbara Charone – an experienced PR who counts the likes of Madonna and Kasabian among her client list.

Cold calling of this style is generally considered bad form, and most showbiz journalists understand the rules. Which is why these visits to the family home seem out of sync with an experienced music or celebrity reporter seeking out a fresh angle on all those *X Factor* rumours.

'I've signed the contract and the news is being announced tonight, officially, so it could be something to do with that,' he says. 'But I just don't know...'

The penny drops. There's a slim chance a more personal narrative might be at play, a story involving his estranged twin, Ben.

'I think it's nastier,' he says. 'I think it's gonna be about my brother...'

He begins to explain his theory. With his nan's passing somebody might be stirring things up regarding the family dispute with Ben.

'OK, so obviously if it were anything about me then they wouldn't be hassling my parents over it – or my sister – would they?' he says. 'They'd come straight to me and say, "Is it true about this? Is it true about that?" That's how the press do it, you know what I mean? They obviously want more information on that situation [regarding Ben's distance from the family]. Mum and Dad, and my sister, have never spoken to the press about this. They wouldn't. It saddens them...'

He knows that hearing the news about the family loss second hand would have upset Ben, but according to Olly reaching out has so far proved impossible. His home address, email and phone numbers are currently a mystery.

'But that's because of *him*. His exact words were, "I don't want to be a part of the family anymore."'

As he talks, Olly becomes more agitated.

'Why doesn't he just get in contact?' he says. 'He knows where we live. Just pick up the phone, or come round and actually talk about it. Or justify it. Not even justify it. Ask my dad, "Look, I know we don't talk anymore, but I know Nan died and I'd like to go to the grave and pay my respects."'

It upsets Olly that his high-profile career can sometimes impact upon the family in this way. He knows this situation wouldn't be unfolding in such an unpleasant fashion if it weren't for his fame, and the media intrusion that constantly orbits him. His mum, he says, doesn't want to publicly discuss the feud that split Ben from his family. 'That's someone she gave life to, she brought him into this world. It's not a nice thing to talk about.'

Faye is a victim, too. She's also lost contact with her brother in the fallout. 'My sister, bless her, is very paranoid about things like this. It'll freak her out for a couple of weeks…'

He gets angrier. 'It's my nan! So my dad informed me that my nan died – why have I got to pick up the phone and ring *him*? My dad didn't contact my brother because he has no way of contacting him. So what do you do as a family? You can't do anything! No one knows where he is. No one knows where he lives…'

Can you resolve it?

'I don't know,' he says. 'I can't answer that. I'm really annoyed today, more so because it makes me uneasy. Why are people doing that? Why would someone be knocking on my parents' door, and my sister's door? It makes no sense…'

—

There's another downside to Olly's job: he occasionally worries about the public and how they view him.

'I do,' he says. 'Because people's perceptions change. I'm a nice guy, I'm a regular guy. I'm like everyone else. I like to have a good time and a good laugh. Very rarely – touch wood – is there a negative story about me. The only thing they seem to drag up is my brother. Like I said, it's the only black mark against my name.'

When he says 'they', he's referring to the national press.

You see it as a black mark?

'It's just because it's got my name tagged to it,' he says. 'It's the only part of my life that isn't perfect and they can twist on that.'

Olly settles himself. He knows tonight's show will be a chance to release some tension, to forget the stress.

'As long as these stories, or these negatives, don't turn people against me, and people don't read it and go, "You were really out of order for not talking, and missing your brother's wedding," and all that crap… That was my worry when it all came out.'

—

Recently Olly watched a tour documentary on the US singer, Katy Perry. During filming, a painfully intimate moment was captured among the grim heartbreak surrounding her split with comedian, Russell Brand. Perry was about to go onstage. She appeared emotionally distraught – 'In tears, in bits,' says Olly. 'But she still got up there and nailed the performance. She shut it all out.'

He can understand Perry's compartmentalisation of pain. No matter what's happening in his personal life, he can often localise the stress and the worry so it's hidden away from his audience. He wants the show to operate at full tilt, no matter what's eating away at him emotionally – like today.

'I always get up there with the idea that I have to put a smile on everyone's face,' he says. 'Some of the people in the audience might be going through tough times themselves. They might have lost someone, or had a terrible week. One of my songs might be helping them through a break-up. There's no way I'm going out there to do a show half-hearted.'

—

Olly emerges for the encore dressed in a kilt, plus sporran, which seems ironic given his final song of the night is 'Wrapped Up'. He walks stage front. The first row starts to chant.

'*Off! Off! Off!*'

It spreads to the back within seconds. Soon the whole arena is chanting.

'*Off! Off! Off!*'

He starts to laugh. 'I'm not going to show you guys what's going on underneath! No, no, no!'

He shushes the crowd. There's an announcement to make.

'Glasgow, Scotland,' he shouts. 'I wanna say a few things. Thank you so much for the love and support, I really mean it from the bottom of my heart.

Thank you all so much for coming tonight, it really is amazing. I've got such great support here. I love coming up here and seeing you guys. You all enjoy the show?'

There's a huge roar. He takes a second to soak in the love and the noise.

'Listen, I'm really excited about the rest of 2015. I hope you guys are excited, too. I'm excited about releasing some new music. I'm also excited about potentially being on TV... what do you reckon? Would you guys like me to be in your living rooms every Saturday night?'

There's another huge cheer.

'Well maybe, just maybe, you might have some confirmation when you get home. Who knows? But listen, I love you all very much. Have a great night, a safe journey home. Stay cheeky, keep smiling... good night and god bless.'

—

X Factor's official twitter account has announced Olly's appointment:

NEWSFLASH: @ollyofficial and @carolineflack1 are officially the new presenters of #XFactor!

Maybe now the speculation and intrusion will stop – for a little while, at least – though that's the least of his concerns as he clambers into the people carrier.

'I bloody shrivelled up under that kilt,' he laughs.

—

Olly doesn't like to hang around after shows. There's rarely a backstage drinking session, or the revelry enjoyed by some bands after gigs. Instead he prefers to locate his hotel room as quickly as possible, avoiding the chasing cars, full of fans, that often trail him home. It's not been five minutes since he departed the stage with Mark and Mellissa, but already a crush of girls are waiting for him at the gates of the backstage car park. As his people carrier slows in traffic, Tony, who sits up front, counts seven cars giving chase to Loch Lomond, where his band have taken up base for four days.

'Have we got followers?' says Mark.

The driver nods. 'When we pulled out they were parked on the left and the right,' he says. 'We'll lose them.'

Mark has to brief Olly on another security development.

'OK, Oll, going forward from the next hotel you are now checked in as Sam Crow, OK? They're all over your last false name...'

Pseudonyms have long been a security precaution for pop stars checking into hotels, where fans will happily knock on doors and ring through to bedside telephones in the middle of the night. Olly's latest name has been taken from the fictional Hell's Angels motorcycle club as portrayed in US TV show, *Sons Of Anarchy* (it's an acronym: Sons of Anarchy Motorcycle Club, Redwood Original).

'They've got Jaime Lannister already?' says Olly. He sounds annoyed. He liked his previous pseudonym – it came from the TV show, *Game of Thrones*.

'That's because someone's told them the names we're checked in under. It does my head in.'

'What? The names you're booked in at reception?' says Mellissa, offering him a eucalyptus wipe for his brow. He's still sweating.

Olly nods. 'Yeah, they'll call up and say, "Oh, is Olly Murs there?" And someone will say, "No, but he's booked in under Jon Snow, or Jaime Lannister, or whatever name we're using…"'

'This is the third time already,' says Mark. 'We can deal with it, we've just got to keep the ball moving. There are passwords in place for everything. I went through a full security check with the hotel today… But listen, if they want to follow us all the way out here just to watch Olly walk into a lift, then fair play to 'em.'

—

Rob, his personal trainer, is along for the ride. Olly reluctantly eats a banana and sips on a pint glass filled with iced coconut water. 'You've gotta re-energise and rehydrate,' says Rob, almost mantra-like.

Olly grimaces with every mouthful. 'It tastes like… something I'm not gonna say,' he says.

'It's all good for you, man,' says Mark.

'I'm only doing it because Rob's here. Last week it was McDonald's and Big Macs all the way,' says Olly. 'That KFC bucket we had the other day was amazing. It was a family-sized one. We all had a bucket each and we played a game to see who could eat the bones first. Bloody boring this car journey.'

—

Twitter is his instantaneous barometer – for good news and bad. Olly's feed is currently going crazy. Following his onstage announcement and *X Factor*'s confirmation on Twitter, messages and texts of congratulations flood in. He scrolls through his phone, checking for comments.

Olly laughs. 'David Walliams just texted me. He's written, "Congratulations you big gay bastard!"'

He begins to consider some new catchphrases for the show.

'How about, "Your Saturday night just got better! Just sit back and relax while me and Caroline take on you a fest of awesomeness. Everything you need is right here!"'

'Isn't that a bit like saying you're better than Dermot?' says Mellissa.

'No, it's saying, "Your Saturday night just got better, turn off *Strictly*..."'

Mark has a brainwave. 'You know what? You could take that line out of "Uptown Funk"...'

Olly mulls it over. '"It's Saturday night, we're in the spot. Don't believe me? Just... *watch*!" Yeah, and I'll have Bruno Mars calling me every week.'

His phone buzzes again. It's a public note from *X Factor*'s departing warm-up guy, Ian Royce. For over a decade, it's been Royce's job to entertain studio audiences at ITV before the live shows have started. Olly reads his letter aloud.

'It says, "I am gutted because I won't get to warm up two lovely people whose hearts met through a TV show I love and care for as I do my own child. Having said that, I'm overjoyed and proud of two people I love and respect very much now that 11 years of my life on *X Factor* will be driven by two talented, passionate, beautiful, loving, caring, real stars. They're the best choice ever. Go shine your amazing double act. I'll watch with pride on every level. Time for a hashtag BOOM!"'

There's also been a tweet from Dermot, the man Olly's set to replace.

'Huge congratulations to Olly and Caroline. Please be gentle with the old girl... That's the show, not Louis Walsh.'

—

He's played the first of three Glasgow shows in a row, experienced what could be an unfolding tabloid drama and announced, officially, *finally*, his new role on *X Factor*. It was quite a hectic day, even by Olly's standards, but as he sits in his dressing room the following afternoon, the emotional strain has barely dented him. It rarely does these days.

There are few concerns about burnout, or the idea that he might be spreading himself too thin – mentally and physically. The fear of fatigue doesn't bother him either; he's been through what he describes as an episode of depression once before, a result of overdoing it both at work and play, and he knows how to spot the warning signs. His trainer is also a constant reminder of what not to do – 'Don't go out drinking, don't go out partying. They're the things that have kept me alright. I feel good at the moment,' he says.

Olly knows how to keep his mood upbeat, but you only need to Google his name to discover what can happen when he overworks himself. The details arrive halfway down the first page of search results in a *Daily Mail* feature entitled, ominously, 'I was a zombie. Drinking too much, depressed, crying: Olly Murs on the darker side of fame.'

In it, he explains how he 'totally lost the plot'. There's talk of excess pressure, inexperience and worry. Working 16 hours a day in the public eye, seven days a week: the workload soon took a heavy toll. Though his symptoms seemed more in tune with exhaustion and pressure rather than a psychological meltdown.

'I couldn't handle it, but I couldn't admit that to myself, let alone anyone else,' he admitted in the paper. 'Thinking about it now, it was like I'd got the chance to have everything I wanted and I was terrified by it. It just built up and up. In the end I was sitting in a meeting and I just started crying.

'I don't think my management knew up until that point what was going on. I burst into tears and they told me to take a break. It's crazy but that was the last thing I expected to hear. I almost expected them to say, "Well, goodbye then." But they had more faith in me than I had in myself and they also realised I was burnt out. It took two weeks for me to sort myself out.'

Much of the problem stemmed from an overloaded work schedule. Olly was set to release a new album, 2011's *In Case You Didn't Know*. He had been asked to present *Xtra Factor* alongside Caroline Flack. His routine became an intense merry-go-round of photoshoots, interviews, TV filming and recording sessions. There were live shows and public appearances, as well. 'Too much going on,' he said, reflecting on that time.

Talking to me in the dressing room, now, his mood changes. 'I wasn't having a good time, I wasn't happy. I needed a rest, I needed to recharge my batteries, see my mates and get away from the industry. I was a bit depressed. I was nervous about the album coming out. I was nervous about the live show, *Xtra Factor*, because I had no idea how to do live TV. I'd never done it as a presenter before. It was a mind-melt.'

That's when he began drinking. 'Vodka and orange before shows,' he says. 'I always wanted a drink.' He found that alcohol boosted his self-belief. 'You wouldn't associate a lack of confidence with my personality, but I was just in a really intense, nervous state.'

In the end, a two-week holiday was enough to level him out. 'I came back and I was as fresh as a daisy, I got everything done, I smashed it and I was back to normal. The single went to number one, the album went to number one. Then *Xtra Factor* started and it was brilliant, the reviews were great and I was fine.'

His forthcoming schedule sounds worryingly similar to the period that preceded this tricky episode, but Olly's learned from his mistakes. He factors in days of rest while he's on tour; plenty of personal space and FIFA time help, too. When he begins to feel the strain, he talks to Mark or Sarah. Most of all, he's older and more comfortable in his own skin. There's a trust in himself, his achievements and his ambitions.

'I was at the start of my career when it happened, it was a bit different then,' he says. 'I was craving success, massively. I wanted to keep the number ones going, I wanted to maintain that. If the second album had come out and flopped, I wouldn't have done anything else afterwards – I wasn't a big enough name back then. With everything going well, it made me feel a lot better in myself, and about what happened next. I'm a lot more laid back now.

'Yeah, I'm still driven to be successful. I still want to do well. I still want *X Factor* to be the best. I want us to smash it, and I can't wait to get my teeth into it and start working. But I'm at a different place in my career. It won't affect me like that anymore. If I get tired I'll turn round and say, "I'm not doing that, I want a day off. I need a couple of days off to get my head straight, to rest."'

—

It's easy to lose your way when fame first arrives. There is attention at every turn, invitations to parties and events that were previously out of reach. After *X Factor*, Olly visited Simon Cowell's place. 'He lives a very show business life,' says Olly. 'He's huge, he's got loads of money, he goes on all these amazing Caribbean holidays, and fair play to him, he works hard. Simon's a very successful man.' Olly doesn't fancy that lifestyle for himself. 'I think I'm built differently. I'm a different kind of person.'

But as a single lad from Essex with new-found fame and wealth, Olly threw himself in at first. 'I was whisked away,' he says. 'I'd just got famous. Like every lad in that situation I was out clubbing, having the time of my life. Then I realised very quickly, within about three or four months, that it wasn't for me. I needed to get out of that routine very quickly, otherwise it was gonna cause massive problems.

'Every day I was going out and feeling tired, drained; the buzz was wearing off. I needed to focus on getting the first album right and having a number one, before I could start gallivanting around London, drinking everywhere. So I stopped and went to live at home...'

It worked. He stayed with his parents until he was 28 years old. When he moved out he had three albums to his name. Two of them number ones. Only his self-titled debut had been kept off the top spot, and that was by Take That's *Progress*, which later turned out to be the second-fastest-selling UK album of all time. If you're going to finish second, it's not bad to lose out to a near-record breaker.

—

Mark knocks on his dressing room door. There's a meet and greet to deal with, a daily soirée involving competition winners, record label execs and corporate sponsors. He turns off the PlayStation and gathers himself. Sometimes he finds it hard to be Olly Murs: the public face, at the flick of a switch.

'You've always got to be on show,' he says. 'It's mentally draining. Most of the time, I'm not putting a show on, but sometimes I wake up and I can't be arsed to do this. I want to stay in bed. I might have had an argument with someone and I'll think, *I can't be bloody bothered today*. When I walk into a room, I've got to be smiling, happy and going, "Hey! How are you doing?" But being happy with people all day can be mentally tiring, especially when you just want to go to your room, scream at the wall and have a go at someone.'

Most of the time, he tells people that his job isn't hard because he 'loves it'. He also knows it's nowhere near as physically tough as some vocations. 'I'm not on a bloody building site,' he'll say. 'I'm not physically drilling into the ground, or lifting bricks and tarmacking roads – and I know people who do that and it's tough work. So my job isn't physically hard. I do interviews, I do photoshoots, and I can see people saying, "That's not a hard day." But it's hard mentally.'

When pushed, he admits that the only thing he would like more of is a routine in tune with the Monday to Friday nine-to-five that his friends work to. He loves that his life is unpredictable; there's excitement at every turn and he gets a kick out of the not knowing. But a 'normal' weekend every now and then makes for refreshing recuperation.

'I used to like having weekends off,' he says. 'I still do. That's the best time. Friday nights with the boys, Saturday nights with the missus; Saturday afternoon watching the football, playing football on Sunday morning in a local team. A roast dinner with the family. A Sunday night chilling out in front of the TV, watching box sets. It's what weekends are all about.'

It's easy to understand the appeal. With *X Factor* looming into view, quiet weekends will soon be in short supply.

OLLY ON THE RECORD: HAPPINESS

Despite some of the negatives that come with my career, life is great – I see the headlines and stuff as coming with the territory. My job's fun. It's brilliant. And I don't love it because of the money, or the lifestyle, or the fame. I love it because I love music.

I don't like the perception some people have of pop stars, and celebrities, though. They want to think that when I'm not working, when I'm not on tour, or in the studio, I'm sitting on a beach, or somewhere in Monaco, driving around in an F1 racing car, living the dream. But it's nothing like that really.

I want to stay as normal as I can. I know I'm not normal. I know I live a completely different life, and I can't keep saying that I'm normal, but in my head I am. When I want to get in my car and go for a drive, I will. If I want go out to a restaurant, or do some DIY at home, I will. I can't always live a normal life – I know that. But I'll try to live it as normally as I can.

I don't come home to a pool party every day. I could if I wanted, but after a really hard day at work I just want to chill out. Maybe some people in my position live a great life and all that, but listen, there's a lot of people out there that live better lives than musicians; people that are living the dream, and having a great time. And they haven't got the most money in the world either.

Before all this, I travelled Australia with no money. I had the most amazing

time and experience of my life – *ever*. Money couldn't buy me that happiness, and that amazing experience. Money can't buy me the experience of walking out onstage. That's not about money.

I'm having a great time and I'm enjoying everything because of the music and the fans. Like the song says, 'I've never been better'. I know a lot of people out there have taken inspiration from that song. They get a more positive spin on life from it. The chorus is, 'Everybody cries, but not today, Because I've never been better.' That's how I feel right now.

Chapter Eight

PICTURES OF ME

PICTURES OF ME

Sometimes on the *Never Been Better* tour, serious issues resolve themselves. Or, at least, they are concluded away from Olly's sightlines. By the time he's departed the stage in Glasgow a second time, having lifted his kilt to reveal a pair of St Andrew's Cross underpants, Tuesday's stresses and paranoid episodes have been settled. The reporter knocking on his mum's door was located by management and told to submit a less intrusive interview request. Twenty-four hours on, Olly doesn't seem too bothered. He reckons he's already over it.

'We obviously think they're trying to dig something up, or put something together,' he says. 'We don't know anything yet, but my mum and dad are fine, they're on their guard. Anyway, it'll all come out eventually – whatever it is.'

The story will remain unannounced for the rest of the tour, not that Olly would busy himself looking for any negative headlines anyway. He tends to lose contact with the outside world when he's on the road (despite their texts, he says he still hasn't called his mum since the tour started, even though he's been away from home for over two weeks now), and most of the time he's oblivious to what's going on outside the touring bubble, apart from the football headlines. When he wanders into the crew canteen for dinner, he'll sometimes pick up a newspaper. His first move is to scan the sport and showbiz sections. Checking the front pages only depresses him.

'Because the news is usually so horrible,' he says. 'It puts me in a mood where I'm thinking, *Wow, do I really wanna watch what's happening around the world? All these horrible things that are going on...*'

Darren nods. 'He was very grateful for the opportunity. He wanted to work it as much as he could. But he had an undertone of confidence that he probably didn't really know he had himself.'

They've since become friends. John even joined Olly for his thirtieth birthday celebrations last year, a five-day trip on a tour bus to four European countries – France, Sweden, Denmark and Norway. 'We had a mad time,' he says. 'Drinking non-stop from the crack of dawn until we fell asleep. You can hate your boss, or you can get on with your boss. But we're mates with ours.'

Despite the duo's strong vocal unity (Darren and John are best friends; they've always worked together), they're yet to sing on Olly's studio output. That job is left to those vocalists hired by his songwriting team. Every now and then, though, whenever the band hooks up for a promotional show, Olly might ask them for some advice on a song he's writing.

'He's always putting out his ideas to people,' says Darren. 'You can't deny him that because it seems to be working.'

—

For Paul and Mike, the earliest realisation that they had joined a very different brass trio arrived in 2012, following the first arena tour in support of Olly's second album, *In Case You Didn't Know*. As a thank you for their work, the nine-piece (there were only two backing vocalists then) were taken away for a six-day holiday to Las Vegas. The party stayed in the salubrious Caesars Palace casino. They later booked a helicopter ride that swooped them over the Grand Canyon.

Paul laughs. 'Vegas is designed to make you go crazy...'

'That doesn't happen with artists, though,' says Mike. 'He took us away, flights, accommodation, there were 13 of us in total, with Olly, Mark and one or two others. We had a riot. It was like being away with the best bunch of mates. We've always said this in the band, if we ever had to share rooms, there's nobody that you couldn't feel comfortable with.'

Paul remembers experiencing some concerns about his career prospects when first joining Olly's touring band. He feared their initial theatre tour might

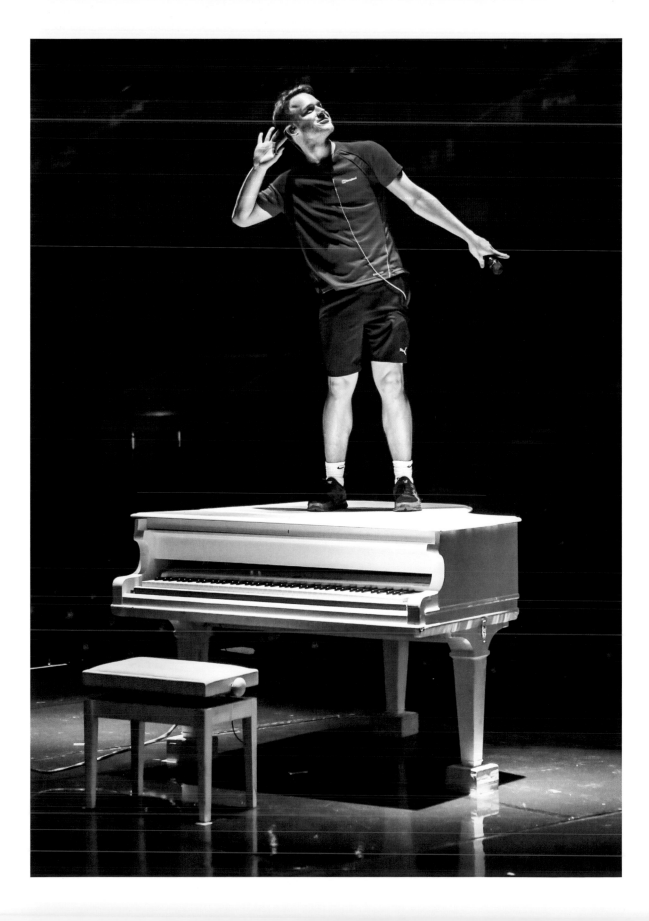

be a one-off. 'I said to my mum, "A lot of these *X Factor* artists don't last very long." She said, "Just enjoy it. You never know." The fact that it's carried on has been ridiculous. There were summer shows, a JLS support... and a lot of the original band are still here.'

Both Paul and Mike met Olly, along with Sarah and Mark, in a London cafe before being recruited. When recalling that first meeting, Paul describes Olly as being not too detached from his onstage or TV persona – 'Geezer-ish. A cheeky chappy. You know, when people ask me what he's really like, I tell them, "Exactly as he is on the telly."'

This matey camaraderie often extends to travelling commitments. When Olly and his band supported Robbie Williams on his Take The Crown Stadium Tour, both touring parties had enough people to put together an 11-a-side football team. Often the stadiums they were playing at had training pitches. Matches were organised. Local football celebrities would often join in the fun.

'In Copenhagen, the former United keeper, Peter Schmeichel came along to watch,' says Rupert, Olly's guitarist. 'And another time, the former Aston Villa manager, Alex McLeish was the referee. We even had our own kits. We had a great team, but sometimes it got feisty with Robbie's lot, which was a bit crazy because we'd have to do a gig that same night. Someone would often say, "Come on lads, calm down. We've got to go to work later..."'

—

Whenever Olly thanks his band onstage, special attention is often paid to his drummer, Dexter – one of the newest members of the touring party.

'When you're younger, you think your name's pretty cool, don't you?' Olly will announce after the show's piano medley. 'You think, "If ever I get famous, I've got a pretty cool name." You might even write it down, and think, "Yeah, that's gonna look pretty good in the paper." But this geezer has got a pretty amazing name. The best name ever, and this is not even a joke, by the way. Ladies and gentlemen: Dexter... Ricardo... Hercules...'

Dexter laughs. 'I used to hate my name,' he says. 'I love it now, though. He first did it when we did an ITV show and my mum was loving it.'

He says the band can tell when Olly's having a good show. He'll wander back along the catwalk towards his microphone with a reassuring nod. "He'll look at me a certain way and I know: it's time to go..."'

—

It's a Friday night in Newcastle. The band have moved their drinking into a Quayside pub. There is talk of a curry; Dexter will later join up with a friend's stag party. Some of the fans are here, too. They've recognised Olly's tour bus, but given he's staying in another residence, out of town, they soon lose interest and go home.

'We want to make those guys happy though,' says John. 'But the challenge comes at the start of the gig, when you see someone miserable, someone who's probably not come to enjoy the show. A lot of blokes are forced to go with their missus, but at the end of it, you can see they've had a great time. That's about us – the band and Olly – winning them over.'

Paul nods. 'I'll defy anyone to come to a gig on this tour and not enjoy themselves. It's just a shame I'll never get to see it from the crowd.'

—

Two days later, before his second show in Newcastle, Olly pays a visit to the Teenage Cancer Trust Unit at The Great North Children's Hospital, a ward that cares for ill kids between the ages of 13 and 18. It's a commitment he doesn't want to publicise in advance. Like a lot of musicians and actors, Olly does plenty of charitable work, but any money he donates, and the time he gives, is his business. Besides, nobody wants to look like they're exploiting a charitable group as part of a grotesque marketing stunt. So today's stop-off is a low-key affair, as is much of the work he's been doing on tour with the kids' charity Brainwave. In addition to his efforts as a patron, he's often provided the charity with free VIP tickets to shows on this tour, meeting his guests backstage before stage time.

Nobody outside of the patients at The Great North Children's Hospital and their families has been alerted to his arrival. Today, the absence of fans and photographers hanging around for his people carrier to pull up – whatever hotel, venue or restaurant that might be – makes for a comforting change. When Olly and Sarah stroll into the foyer, the only person waiting to greet them is Angie Jenkinson, the Trust's music relations manager. Mark has also travelled with the party, but he's decided to wait in the car. He gets too upset when walking through the wards alongside Olly.

'I used to be able to handle it,' he says, shaking his head. 'But now I've got kids of my own... I dunno, I find it heartbreaking.'

Inside, a nurse talks Olly through the facilities, explaining what amenities and social activities the kids can rely upon when they stay here. The plan is for him to pop inside each bedroom to spend time with the patients; they can hang out and chat. 'I'm looking forward to meeting them,' he says, before stopping to sign some autographs for the nurses on reception. There are selfie opportunities, too. A teenage girl, in the ward to visit her brother, jumps up and gives him a kiss on the cheek as they snap a photo. In doing so, she leaves a bright red lipstick mark on his white jumper. She looks mortified.

'Oh no!' he laughs. 'What's my girlfriend gonna say?'

Another girl asks Olly about his voice and whether he likes musicals. 'Have you ever seen *Annie*?' she says.

'Nah,' laughs Olly, pulling a face. 'When I was a kid, I was too busy watching hardcore action movies.'

There's a more pressing request. One of the nurses asks if he could make a short video for a young girl who was staying on the ward. She's currently in intensive care.

'Her name's Emily,' she explains, introducing him to the girl's parents and handing him a phone.

'OK, no problem... Emily... Emily...' he lifts up the phone and presses record. A broad grin appears on his face. 'Hi Emily! Olly here! I've been hunting around for you on the ward, but you're not about. Listen, stay strong, keep smiling...'

He pulls the parents close. 'I'm standing here with your mum at the moment.' He gives her a hug and blows a kiss into the camera.

'Stay safe, darling,' he says, waving.

Emily's mum starts to cry. This could be the most important video message he makes all tour.

—

It's interesting to see a different focus in Olly. His mood in the hospital is reserved. He talks in the cautious, hushed tones used by people whenever they're fearful of being too intrusive, or insensitive, but there's still an upbeat determination about him. It's the side of his personality that wants to please people, the same one his fans experience whenever he's onstage. The showmanship is at work, it's just being delivered in a different way. It's Olly: upbeat, but dialled down.

'I'm against going in, being sad for people,' he says. 'The kids don't want that. They want people to walk in and be positive and upbeat, and talk to them on a level. They don't want pity. They know what they're going through, they deal with it every day, they battle it every day. For me to come in and go, "Oh I'm really sorry." Or, "I hope everything goes OK…" That's not what *I'd* want. I just try to be as positive as I can. Give them a laugh and a joke.'

—

Olly meets Michael, who's been receiving chemotherapy recently. He spots the Xbox positioned at the end of the bed.

'What you playing, Michael?' says Olly. 'If ever I see the Xbox lying around, I've got to have a go.'

Michael shows him the latest edition of Grand Theft Auto. Olly's face lights up.

'Mate, I love GTA! I got to the second level and I had to give up. It was so tough. How are you getting on with it?'

They sit and talk computer games for a while – the 2015 edition of FIFA is a favourite for both of them; he mentions the duels he's been having backstage with Mark on the American football title, Madden NFL.

Sarah has been watching Olly as he moves from bedroom to bedroom, patient to patient. She's been doing these visits for as long as he has, but she finds it harder to summon a brave face.

'He never shows any upset in front of these kids,' she says. 'He acts normally, even though he finds it really sad. Olly just wants them to forget they're ill...'

—

Upstairs, in a college-style common room overlooking Newcastle United's vast football ground, St James' Park, 20 or so patients have gathered to meet Olly, where they can grab autographs, take pictures and chat music for a little while. Along the walls are various instruments donated by artists – drum kits and microphones. Pride of place is a guitar signed by former Oasis singer, and Beady Eye frontman, Liam Gallagher. There's even a vintage jukebox. As Olly walks around the group, chatting to everyone individually, he spots one boy wearing a pair of fancy new trainers.

'Wow! Looking awesome!' he says, pointing at his feet.

The boy beams proudly. 'We'll go on the pull tonight, if you want, Olly.'

He laughs. 'Sorry mate, I've got a girlfriend... But I'll make a good wingman for you.'

—

The people carrier takes him back to Newcastle's Metro Radio Arena. There are no meet and greets today, his box of VIP programmes have been signed. The timetable is free of press commitments. Only FIFA time and dinner mark his schedule. Backstage, he begins to reflect upon his afternoon at The Great North Children's Hospital.

'It never gets easy,' he says, slumping on his sofa. 'And when I have kids it'll be harder to do things like that ...'

Why?

'Because it'll put it more into perspective, you know? With the parents. The only thing I can compare that to is my little nephew, Louie, but even though I love him to bits, he's not *my* child. It's a different kind of bond and a relationship. You see a lot of parents there, and they're happy to see you, but you can tell in their eyes that they're so upset, and they're going through a lot themselves.'

Do these visits affect you afterwards?

'I dunno, I think it will... I've only really had to look after myself in life,' he says. 'Obviously, I've got a great family, and people around me, and that question, if you were to ask me in ten years' time, when I have my own kids...'

He seems to be reaching for a handle on how he'll feel, an answer that won't come across as being overly sentimental, or patronising.

'It's tough being around them and knowing what they're going through. Sure, most of the time, they're not in a great place, and they're asking for the reasons about why it's happening to them. When I walk away from the experience...'

He stops.

'Why am I saying "*the experience*"? What am I talking about? I feel so weird when I chat about it. I say it was "fun" to meet the kids but, on the other hand, I feel bad because I know what they're going through. I don't really know how to explain it, or talk about it. I just *deal* with it.

'Yeah I'm meeting these kids and they're going through something really bad, but I don't want them to feel like I can't be mates with them or that I've got a problem with them. I want it to be an organic, or natural thing. A chat.'

But it was like that today though, wasn't it?

'I walked away from it thinking that the kids were so positive, and so happy, and they were really amazing. I felt they were quite bubbly; there were some great characters. Some shy, some not. It was a really positive room, some really positive families. It was exhilarating.'

Some days, though, are clearly tougher than others – even when they're fun.

OLLY ON THE RECORD: THE TEENAGE CANCER TRUST

Working with foundations like The Teenage Cancer Trust is not part of my job, but it's something that I want to do. I want to be able to give something back to charity. I feel that, because of the position I'm in, if I can help kids and help people by using my name, or getting other people involved, or encouraging more people to donate, then it can only be a positive thing.

If I can help just one person by visiting a ward then it's amazing. If I can help hundreds, or even thousands, then it's even better. It's about trying to help people as much as I can because if I ever found myself in that position, I'd want people to help me. Right now, I'm privileged to be in a great job, but I'm privileged to have a clean bill of health, too. I know that could change at any moment. My friends have lost loved ones to cancer. I know how important the treatment is.

What I take away from these visits is how much positivity there is with the doctors and the environment. The Teenage Cancer Trust has it spot on – it's a fun place for the kids to be in, regardless of the stress, and the worries, and the anxieties of what they're going through. The children form great friendships with other people in there. It helps them to get through a tough time by communicating with other kids. They get to realise that it's not just them in that situation. They can all relate. And that's so important.

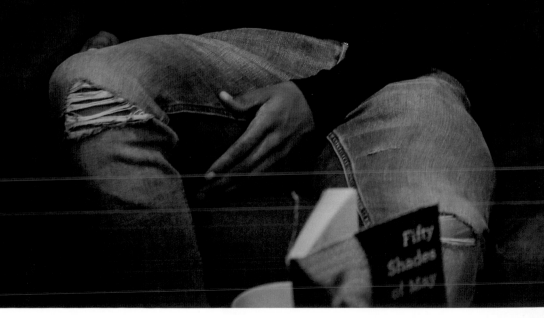

Chapter Nine

UNITED
WE STAND

UNITED WE STAND

On the afternoon before his opening show in Manchester, Olly decides to take a sunbed session, his sixth of the tour. Mark wants to prevent a fan-related scrum, so he books a salon located 20 minutes away from the city centre. For extra security, Olly is again checked in as Sam Crow, his longest-running hotel pseudonym of the tour so far. It's hoped a crush of fans won't be waiting for him outside the shop, which is tucked away on a suburban side street, though any hopes of a low-key arrival are dashed once he enters the salon. As Olly signs the register (he scribbles his own name), latest single 'Up' – his recently released duet with Demi Lovato from *Never Been Better* – is introduced on Radio 1, which just so happens to be the salon's station of choice.

'What are the bloody odds?' groans Mark under his breath.

The receptionist glances down at her signing-in book and cocks a thumb towards the speakers.

'Er, not being funny, but is this...?'

Before she has a chance to finish her sentence, Olly confirms his identity with a laugh and a sheepish shrug.

'Yeah, bit awkward,' he says. Later he will point out to Mark that this hardly represents his most excruciating case of bad timing. 'A couple of years ago I had a car accident in Harlow, Essex. I was about to meet a mate for lunch and I hit some ice. My Fiat skidded straight into a central reservation and – *boom!* – my car was completely wiped out. I was devastated.'

Apparently, another driver at the scene had witnessed the accident. He stopped to exchange contact details, which is when the embarrassment began.

'I said to him, "OK, the last thing I want is for anyone to recognise me, or to ask for pictures. I'm mortified this has happened. Let me get your numbers and stuff..." So I get to the door of my car, reach down for a pen and at the same time, "Thinking Of Me" comes on the stereo. We both just looked at each other and started laughing.'

—

Half an hour later, Olly is surveying his skin tones. He doesn't look impressed.

'What's the point?' he says, rubbing at the colour on his arms. 'I'm not doing that again. I usually get a spray tan but it runs off during shows. I'm supposed to get some colour with the sunbed, to look good, but...'

He gives his forearm another dismissive wipe. 'Never again...'

'Yeah man,' says Mark, looking over at him. 'Embrace your true colour – pale.'

Olly stares down at his not-quite-tanned skin and sighs.

—

In the Manchester Arena, he begins talking about how hard he likes to work. To prove his point, Olly uses various items lying around the dressing room as props. First up, a granola bar.

'Right, if you said to me, "Olly I need you to put these biscuits into a box, and you need to fill 300 boxes," I'd do it to the best of my ability. I'm a hard worker. Whenever I do something, I work on it, 110%.'

He gestures to the empty seats outside his door in the venue, all 15,000 of them, currently empty. 'Or, if you said, "Olly, I need you to do a 50-date arena tour," then I'd give it 110%, every night.'

He stands up, now animated. There's another example coming. '"Olly, I need you to do a paper round, twice a day. I have 50 customers in the morning, 50 in the evening..."'

But there's a twist. '"... *for the next five years*." I'd do it perfectly, no problem. I've never had a bad job, and I've never been sacked. I've never had a bad reference from any company that I've ever worked at because I always give it everything.'

His updated schedule has prompted this display. The weekend's itinerary has arrived from Mark, and it's full. In addition to the usual meet and greets, programme signings, training workouts, and several promo interviews, there's an *X Factor* advert to film, plus a televised interview with MUTV – the official channel for Olly's team, Manchester United. His last commitment requires a trip to Carrington, the club's salubrious training ground. 'The home of football,' he announces proudly, scanning Mark's email for a second time. He notes there's also a charity dinner to attend, one football match (Everton against United; a private box has been booked), plus the small matter of three sold-out shows at the Manchester Arena.

Of all Olly's commitments in the coming days, it's tomorrow's trip to Carrington that has him fired up the most. 'I'm a big fan,' he says, pointing to the United bag sitting on a table. 'But I sometimes get people slagging me off because I'm not actually from the city, though that doesn't happen a lot. I've been to away games, in the crowd with the fans, and they love it. They know I'm there to watch the greatest team in England...'

It's not just United's fans that are increasingly accepting of his celebrity status. His relationship with the bloke in the street has also changed. In the early stages of his career, Olly was occasionally targeted by blokes, 'getting aggro'; jealous boyfriends of the girls trailing him to shows. 'There'd be idiots who'd cause problems,' he says. 'It was a tough time. Lads can get threatened quite easily by another geezer, especially if he's famous and their girlfriend likes him.'

There were occasions when the trouble threatened to escalate from sarcastic jokes and comments into violence. 'But when you're out drinking, you're always gonna get some clown,' he says. 'There's always some idiot out there who wants to cause a fight, whether you're famous, or not.'

He recalls a skirmish that took place one Christmas, a couple of years back. Olly and several friends had organised a party at a bar with a table-tennis room. The idea was to have a drink and play a few games, but as the group took up a table, somebody from a nearby party threw a handful of ping-pong balls in their direction. At first, everyone ignored the interruption – *Whatever*, thought Olly. Then shortly after several more were thrown.

'Me being me, I don't care,' he says. 'I don't have that attitude of being scared of anyone. So I said, "What are you playing at? Why are you throwing stuff at us? It's not that funny. Sod off. Leave it. Go and enjoy your night, and let us enjoy ours. Please don't cause any problems."'

Olly explains how, when their game resumed, another handful of balls was hurled towards them. He walked over again. 'I said, "Mate, what are you doing? I just saw you do it again. Seriously. We're trying to have a nice game of table tennis here..."' Then his friends came over. 'One of them says, "Who do you think you are?" I thought, *Oh, here we go...*'

Olly refused to back down. 'I was like, "Do yourself a favour. You do not want to get into a row – go away." I said, "I'm not trying to be a big man, I don't want to get in a fight with you." In the end, one of their group – a really nice bloke, to be fair – smoothed it over. It sounds a trivial story, I know, but you never know what might happen in a situation like that. It's something me and my mates have to deal with every now and then, I guess. Sometimes, some random blokes just want to antagonise me for a laugh.'

He reckons the threats and antagonistic comments are rare these days. Most people want to buy him a beer rather than hurl a ping-pong ball in his direction. A lot of that has to do with his blokey appeal – the appearances in charity football matches like Soccer Aid, the good humour in which he took several public pranks played on him by TV presenters Ant and Dec. In 2015, Olly even topped the leader board on *Top Gear*'s 'Star in a Reasonably Priced Car'. The challenge, a popular feature on the BBC2 car show, had seen celebrities as famous as Tom Cruise and Cameron Diaz racing a Vauxhall Astra around a test track. Olly leapfrogged the field with his record time. 'I hadn't felt a buzz like that in ages,' he says of the performance.

While he's understanding of why the hassles have diminished, he's also familiar with why they happened in the first place. Jealousy and insecurity are feelings he occasionally experiences himself, even now.

'Francesca still fancies other singers, even though I'm famous,' he says. 'She talks about models she likes, Hollywood actors. I'm like, "Alright! What are you talking about him for?" It happens all the time, but it doesn't mean I'm gonna take it any further. I'm not gonna go out and find that geezer.'

—

His friend James Mace, or Mace, has joined the touring party for a few days. The plan is for them to hang out, go to a party after his final show in Manchester and watch some football together, though this is as much for Mace's benefit as Olly's. It's his late mum that's being affectionately referenced during the onstage introductions to 'Dear Darlin''. A few days on tour, reckons Olly, will be a good distraction for the pair of them. 'So I won't be doing the whole "Dear Darlin'" chat when I play tonight,' he says.

This arrival should create a bit of normality within the touring bubble, but as with everything Olly does on tour, even a few days of matey high jinks becomes amplified. The first step on their itinerary is the trip to Carrington to meet England international, Ashley Young as part of his interview on MUTV. It's hardly your typical lad's day out, though this is less a thrill for Mace as it is Olly – like Mark, he's a Liverpool fan. The intense rivalry triggers a three-way argument during the car journey to Manchester United.

'Sir Alex Ferguson is someone that knows a bit more about football than you, Oll!' shouts Mark as the conversation becomes more animated.

'What are you chatting on about?!' snaps Olly. 'Oh Mark, open your eyes, you're a deluded Liverpool fan.'

Mace looks at his watch. The bickering has lasted for 25 minutes, so far. It only ends when the people carrier pulls into United's car park.

—

Olly settles onto the TV studio sofa next to Ashley Young and asks about United's season. There's a brief discussion about the dressing room playlist before matches (Dutch house is very popular, apparently). Presenter Helen McConnell asks Olly about the times he's played football at Old Trafford – he's appeared there three times during charity games. 'Is it better than being on tour?' she says.

'I'm telling you now, 100% it is,' he says.

'I thought you were going to say no!' she laughs.

'I've been lucky to play there, like in the United Legends game. But the best one was last year, [Chelsea manager] José Mourinho came off the bench and took me out on the pitch with a kick.' He's right, too. A later scan of YouTube shows the Chelsea manager swiping at Olly's ankles during the Soccer Aid match. The tackle put a confused Olly on his backside. The clash was so memorable it later made it into Premier League rhetoric.

'I remember Mourinho did a press conference just before a Chelsea v Man U game this season,' explains Olly in the studio. 'He was asked how he was going to tackle our players and he goes, "I am going to do to them what I did to Olly Murs – I am going to take them out." I was sitting there watching *Sky Sports News* going, "Get in! Get in!"'

—

Olly kicks a ball outside for photos and signs autographs. He tries out equipment in the club gym. When he gets back into the people carrier with Mark and Mace, the arguing starts again.

'Do you watch *Match of the Day* when United lose?' yells Mark.

'Yeah, I do,' shouts Olly.

'When they lose?'

'Yes I do!'

Mark goes up in decibels. 'When they *lose*?!'

'Yeah! Yeah I do.'

'You liar!' he declares.

Olly complains that it's like 'being in a school playground' when they talk football. Though the high ground is lost when he begins comparing pop stars to

the world's best footballers. "Gareth Bale trying to be Ronaldo is like me trying to be Bruno Mars. I'm Gareth Bale, Ronaldo is Bruno Mars."

Mace sighs. 'You want to set your sights a bit higher there, mate.'

—

The people carrier arrives at the Manchester Arena. A large crowd of fans, maybe 50 or more, has gathered outside the car park. Tony sets about organising the mob, now cheering and screaming, into an orderly queue. Teenage girls thrust their phones through the gates separating them from the backstage area and Olly. Each one will receive a surreal selfie, their arms and face pushed awkwardly against him through the metal barriers.

'Get your phones ready,' shouts Mark. 'Let's go...'

Olly moves down the line, saying hello and performing his repertoire of long-practised poses: the cheesy grin, a thumbs-up shot; today's favourite is the one

where he pokes his tongue out at a funny angle. Mace stands back from the crowd. This is a scene he's become accustomed to over the last five years.

'At first it was really weird,' he says. 'Before *X Factor* he was never anything special, or a ladies' man. Sometimes you get one guy in a group of lads who's always good with the girls, but he was just a normal bloke. So when it first happened it was like, "Why are all these girls screaming for him? Just because he's done a bit of singing?"'

—

A note is passed into Mark's hand from one of Olly's hardcore fans.

'To Marky! We appreciate everything you do for us as always! Always puts a smile on our faces when we see our cheeky Murs! Tell Tony to smile more... JOKES!

'PS What has he been eating? Getting a 6-pack... WHATTTT!!!'

—

X Factor's production team is already backstage to record a TV advert for their forthcoming season. The idea is to film a promotional clip that they hope will attract contestants to a round of auditions starting next month. Their treatment is typically ambitious, involving behind-the-scenes shots of Olly striding through the venue, surrounded by an entourage of Mark, Mellissa, Tony, plus personal trainer Rob, and Mark's assistant, Jordan. The final 'hero shot' is a planned frame of Olly onstage, his arms spread wide, in front of a packed Manchester Arena, all flashing light bulbs and cries of 'Olly! Olly! Olly!' from the audience. This recording is scheduled to take place after 'Right Place Right Time', his second song of the set. Mark outlines the plan.

'We'll have you dressed for eight, then we'll do the first bit of the filming,' he says. 'This should be finished by 8.15, so you can go back into the dressing room and get in the zone. Then you can go out, do the opening part of the show before the cameras come on.'

Olly begins to read the script aloud, memorising the brief soliloquy. The words neatly summarise his journey from auditioning hopeful to arena headliner.

'This year I'm back on *X Factor*,' he says, pacing backwards and forwards outside his dressing room. '...And I want you to be a part of it. Five years ago, I made an audition and it changed... my life forever? My life forever.'

He checks the script. '*It changed my life forever.* So if you think you've got the X Factor, then we want to meet you, so head to the website and sign up.'

Mark wants to make sure that tonight's recording doesn't impact on the show's momentum. He's worried a delay could alter the mood of the crowd.

'We can't lose what we've got going onstage, Oll,' he says. 'At the end of the day this is your tour and people have paid good money to see you. It's not as if it's an *X Factor* show where people get free tickets.'

Olly pretends to look angry. 'Oi! Don't talk about my TV show like that.'

—

After 'Right Place Right Time', he hypes up the crowd, leading everyone with a call-and-response chant of 'Olly! Olly! Olly!' The fans scream back loudly. Two TV cameras follow him around the stage.

'OK, you might not want to take pictures of me tonight,' he yells, 'but this is the one occasion when I really want you to take a photo with the flash on your phone. Get your phones ready and when I go like this...'

He points to the ceiling. '...I want every single one of you, if you can, to flash your camera. That's all I am gonna ask of you tonight, and then, I promise you, I will take my top off for the ladies!'

Flashbulbs and mobile phones flicker and sparkle around the stadium. As promised, at the close of the evening, he strips down to his waist, flexing his muscles in front of the screaming crowd.

'Good job I've been working out,' he laughs, as he runs offstage.

—

Before his third and final Manchester show, his mum and dad, Vicky and Pete, arrive backstage for dinner. By now, Olly reckons the show is in good enough shape for them to visit, not that they're behind speed on his efforts so far. Although it's their first gig of the tour, they've been following his reviews on Twitter.

'The reports are always brilliant,' says Pete. 'Well, until they get to London. Then it gets a bit critical...'

A small dinner table has been laid out with cutlery, breads, wine, napkins and a menu. Positioned outside Olly's dressing room, it adds enough civility to the sporting-venue-style surroundings backstage for a family get-together.

'I guess they're my biggest critics,' says Olly as they all settle down to eat. 'But to be honest if they had a problem with the performance at this stage there's not a lot I could do about it. I know they're gonna love it though, it's exciting.'

Manchester carries a wider appeal for Vicky and Pete, however. It's from here that most of their favourite bands first originated. 'Like The Smiths, Joy Division, The Fall, The Charlatans,' lists Vicky. 'We've seen Morrissey here, so it's weird to see the stage that we watched him on and then, suddenly, Olly's on it. And to go to the changing rooms and think, *Ooh, Morrissey's been here, in this shower...* It's the nearest I've been to getting his autograph.'

Before dinner starts, Olly has something to show the family. He pulls up his shirt and flexes his abdominals. Pete snorts. 'Oh, shut up, Olly. I'm gonna buy you a new man-boob bra.'

He smiles, recognising the hard work that would have gone into shaping his son's new physique. 'Seriously though, you're looking fit.'

'Yeah, lost a stone,' says Olly, proudly. He glances down at his dad's feet. He's wearing a pair of box-fresh trainers. 'Really? Sneakers at your age?'

There's a bit of a cuddle. 'Leave it out. So how you doing then, boy?' asks Pete, showing parental concern. 'The old tour's getting some good reviews, innit?'

Vicky butts in. 'Doing any Tommy Steele this time? Some Tom Jones?'

Olly laughs, changing the subject quickly. 'Are you gonna come to *X Factor* every week, then?'

'No, why would I go every week?' she says. 'I can watch you on the telly. We used to go when he was singing – do you remember that? We went through each week in 2009, each show, until eventually we thought, *We're in the final!* I think he was the same as well. He didn't ever empty his suitcase when he stayed in the boot camps. It was always there with his clothes still packed, as if he was going home that week.

'The other families were different. They would say, "We're going to the final and we're gonna book our hotels for next week. Have you booked yours?" We always said, "No," because we wouldn't chance fate that way. We just went week to week. Before you knew it, he was there in the last show.'

As if the circumstances surrounding their makeshift meal weren't unusual enough, recalling his reality TV experience has just added an extra layer of the strange.

—

Olly begins vocal warm-ups in his dressing room. A series of ascending notes echo around the backstage area as Vicky and Pete finish their meal.

'I get really nervous,' says Vicky. 'I don't know why because he goes out there and just... does it.'

'I'm not,' says Pete, 'because I can see he ain't nervous.'

Vicky nods. 'I know *he's* not. But I do because we're always in the audience. I often take a step back and look at the seats and think, *Wow, all these people are here to see him.* But when we see him onstage, it's like… I don't know. I don't think I'll ever get over the fact that he's onstage in an arena.'

She thinks the only time she's ever spotted a flicker of stage fright in him arrived when they appeared on a celebrity version of the quiz show, *Who Wants to Be a Millionaire?* 'It was on Mother's Day, a special episode. He was scared. I've never seen him so nervous in all my life. He kept going to me, "Have a drink, Mum. Have a drink." I said to him, "I think you need one." He was really nervous, which made me nervous and we muffed it up so bad. We blew a question for £10,000.'

—

In the dressing room, Olly talks through his upbringing with Vicky and Pete. He's pleased to see them in Manchester; he loves having his parents around, and his sister and her family when they come to shows. But he doesn't need their approval, especially not when he's performing onstage. He reckons he's always been happy and confident in his own company. He's always believed in himself regardless of their opinions.

'I feel like, you've got three children, then there's always gonna be one kid that's more independent than the others.' His sister experienced problems growing up. Olly explains how she was bullied as a kid and had to move schools. His upbringing was comparatively uncomplicated. 'When I was little, I had grommets in my ears because I couldn't hear properly,' he says. 'That's probably as bad as it got with me. I was a healthy kid. I never had any problems with school. I never missed homework. I never got into any trouble, or got into any fights; the police never turned up at our door because of me – not that they did for anyone else in the house. So my parents didn't have to babysit me because I was very mature for my age. I was never a mummy's boy, or a daddy's boy, though. I was just doing my own thing.'

What with production rehearsals, the tour, plus a series of promotional commitments, he's been away from home, his family and a number of his friends for four weeks now, but homesickness hasn't touched him yet – until now.

'I guess I miss home now you've asked me about it,' he says. 'When I'm not talking about it, I don't. When I talk about it, like now, I do.'

He lists the things he'd be doing, were he not about to perform in front of a sold-out audience of 15,000 people. He'd be sitting in the garden most probably, or maybe visiting a mate's house. He might go out with Francesca. Then he settles on a more defined plan.

'I'd have a barbecue at mine, bring all the lads over, bring all the girls over, have some drinks, have a casual afternoon, watch a bit of football, play some music. I miss things like that.'

For all his claims to be happy on the road, Olly's still a home person at heart. When he moved into his five-bedroom Essex house in 2012 – the rewards of his reported £8 million fortune – it wasn't located too far away from where he was brought up in Witham. Everyone was within easy reach – friends and family, plus his favourite restaurants and clubs. 'I know where everything is!' he says proudly.

For some reason he decides to list the places someone could visit, were they to arrive in Witham for the first time. 'If you were to say, "Olly, where's the best places to hang out?" I'd point out all the good coffees shops, and pubs. You want a good roast dinner? Well, I know where that is as well... I'm a walking tour guide for Essex.'

So you're a fan of the place, then?

'I love Witham!' he says. 'I love Essex! I love everything about it. People laugh at me when I say I love it, but I do. I actually *love* where I live. I'm in the country. It's quiet. It's chilled. I'm not scared of anyone there. It's home.'

The only other place he might consider moving to, he says, is Los Angeles, but only temporarily. 'There's the sun, the environment. No one's rushing, no one's bothered. Everyone's living in their own little world. You're left to your own devices. What's not to like about California? It's a fun place, but that doesn't mean that I'd live there permanently, though. I would never jump my roots...'

—

Twenty minutes to go before show time. Olly turns on the sound system in his dressing room. The muscular beats of 'Radioactive', hit single for Las Vegas rock band Imagine Dragons, begins to overpower the conversations taking place outside. Pete shrugs his shoulders. 'We can't exactly ask him to turn the noise down anymore, can we?' he says to Vicky.

OLLY ON THE RECORD: TAKING THE *X FACTOR* JOB

Filming the *X Factor* advert got me thinking about my time on the show. It was amazing. Ridiculous. That experience completely changed my life, without question. Then, at the same time, the programme has changed a lot of people's lives, but ultimately it's what you make of the chances it affords you, and the unique opportunity that counts.

I had to work seriously hard when I finished the show – getting my voice right, putting together my own songs, as well as touring the country. Had I not done that, my first album could have been a flop, and if that had happened I wouldn't be doing this arena tour now. I realised that I had to make the most of the opportunity, so I went for it.

I guess it all depends on the type of person you are. The hard work, the belief, and the willingness to learn and develop were already there for me. It still is. I'm constantly developing in this job. I'm not the finished article, and I don't think I ever will be. I just want to keep on getting better. I want to keep on improving. I want my voice to get better, I want to move better onstage, I want to look better. I want to be able to present on TV. I want to do everything, but that's what I'm like. I'm bored if I'm not busy.

I struggle to have days off – 24 hours where I do nothing. I can't do it. I get restless. I need to do something, otherwise I feel like the world is passing me by and I've wasted a whole day.

That's why the *X Factor* job is something I'm really excited about. I'm not going back for sentimental reasons. I want to develop my career and improve. Part of me knows that it's going to be great being on *X Factor* again; I love the show, everyone knows that. But the other part of it is about pushing my career and having a new challenge.

Have there been any downsides to my time on *X Factor*? Yeah, I had a year or two when people dismissed me as just being a reality TV star, but that's a battle that will always be there, whatever happens. I could make eight albums and they might all go to number one, but it's not going to make a difference. Those voices will always complain. They'll say, 'Oh, that guy came from *X Factor*, a reality show. It's not organic enough for us.' They think I got an unfair leg-up through TV, but that doesn't bother me anymore. I can't win that battle.

Going forward, I want to do as much as I can. And as long as what I'm doing is beneficial for my career, then I'll do it. I wouldn't do the *X Factor* job if I didn't think it was good for me. I'm not doing it for the money, or for the buzz of being on TV every week. I'm doing it because I reckon it'll benefit my music, it'll benefit my confidence, and it'll make me a better presenter. Who knows? I might do *X Factor* and it might be a disaster, but at the end of the day I've got to take the risk.

Chapter Ten

TROUBLE-MAKER

TROUBLEMAKER

There's a raucous after-show party in Manchester following his final night at the Arena. Olly and the band commandeer a private balcony in Premiership footballer hangout du jour, Neighbourhood. They guzzle down brightly coloured cocktails and grab kebabs at 5 a.m. Olly follows this with an afternoon at Goodison Park for the match between Everton and Manchester United (United lose 3–0), and a one-stop show in Leeds. By the time his touring party has reached Birmingham for three nights at the Barclaycard Arena, Olly seems off-colour. His throat is tickling, and he complains of feeling 'a little run down'. Not that you'd notice. His first shows maintain a rowdy tempo, but afterwards he admits to experiencing a strange sensation. At times, songs seemed to pass him by.

'There have only ever been a couple of shows that have ever felt like work,' he sighs, sitting backstage. 'It was like that here a bit, and that was the hardest thing for me. I loved it, but I couldn't wait to get offstage because I didn't feel comfortable. I was ill, I was going through the motions... sort of.'

It takes a lot to diminish Olly's buzz for being onstage, as anyone who knows him will explain. It's what he fusses over the most – performing, the gigs; his preparations and the work surrounding them; how he looks and how he sings. 'I've got the vocals to worry about,' he says. 'I've got where I'm gonna stand onstage to worry about. I've got the pyrotechnics to worry about. I've got my outfit to worry about. Do I look good onstage? Am I dancing the right moves? Where are the cameras? I have to get all that into my head.'

For some artists, creativity is what happens in a recording studio. It's the area where they operate most effectively. For them, taking an album on the road can represent a necessary evil. Especially today, when recording contracts currently deliver such unpredictable financial returns (unless, like Olly, you're operating near the altitudes currently patrolled by the likes of Rihanna, Adele or Take That), touring receipts can offer a profitable return. For Olly, however, songwriting is his admittedly enjoyable means to an end. It's what gives him the opportunities to perform onstage, and to large crowds; it allows him to *show off*. 'It's all about the gig for me,' he says.

You don't think about writing new material, or finding ideas for songs when you're on the road, then?

'Not really. There's a great atmosphere in the studio, you have fun and you can write songs. But I'm all about getting out there, onstage, every day of the week. It's what I love to do. It's where I'm comfortable. It's where I'm supposed to be.'

The work doesn't stop once he's offstage, either. There's often analysis and meetings where improvements to the show are discussed, along with suggested tweaks to songs, though he claims to only keep the counsel of those closest to him within his management team. Even then, there are occasionally feisty debates regarding his onstage routine. His jokes and those moments of crowd interaction often come under scrutiny, which is when Olly gets defiant. While chatting backstage or during his trips in the people carrier between shows, he can get surprisingly tetchy when discussing his control over the live show, and the thought he puts into every gig.

'Listen, if someone's got a constructive thing to say, I'll take it in,' he says. 'But if I feel like someone's stepping on my toes over what I'm doing onstage, then that really infuriates me. Then I'm like, "Hang on a minute, I love doing that part of the show. It's my thing. Whatever you think, you can think. But if there are 15,000 people enjoying it out there, then I don't really give a toss what you think. When I'm onstage with a mic in my hand that's *my* job."

'It really annoys me when people critique me, like management, or the band. I think, I'm the only person up there doing it and I'm better at doing it than you. You guys are good at management decisions and you guys are great musicians, so give me a chance to figure it out for myself.'

Has that happened a lot on this tour?

He nods. 'I know there were certain things that were changed in the show early on...' He says those decisions were collective though, pointing to the crowd-pleasing rush of 'Heart Skips a Beat'. Initially this was performed with an alternative intro. After two shows, it was decided the song's original structure packed a heftier punch. Meanwhile, 'Stick With Me', a track from *Never Been Better*, was thrown out altogether.

'But I think that finally – and this isn't me being arrogant – my team and management, and the people around me, have realised that what I'm doing, and what I'm trying to achieve, is right for *me*. It makes me who I am. [Before] I'm thinking, *Stop trying to change me. I'm not another artist. Listen to what I have to say*. To be fair, for the first time, in all the tours I've done, they've listened.'

This is one of the very few times that Olly has become grumpy during interviews while on tour. 'I get really defensive because it's very personal to me,' he says. 'Performing onstage and doing what I do: if anyone in the camp criticises that, in any shape or form, it upsets me.'

Opinions beyond the team rarely count for much – or so he says. On some days, Olly will claim not to read the reviews he receives from Modest! after shows – 'I don't know why they send them,' he says, echoing the nonchalant statement you often hear from artists when they pretend to be indifferent to public opinion (spoiler: they all read them). Chat to the people around him, though, and a different story emerges. He checks them a lot, and tends to only remember the negative comments. Which is probably why, on some days, he'll suggest that he cares little for the notes of a lone critic. '[But] if 10, 20, 30, 100 people didn't like the show, that would annoy me,' he says.

Other times, Olly will claim to read the think pieces, only to disregard the words. 'Obviously, some people like to hear other people's opinions, but I hate reading any reviews on anything. It might say, "Watched Olly Murs in concert last night and it was rubbish... I'm not really sure about this song, but he did some singles... He did 'Heart Skips a Beat', but he's done that before; dancing around onstage and moan, moan, moan... I wouldn't bother going, it's crap." But then you look on their bio and it says they're a massive rock fan! I think, *Why did you even bother going?*'

The only review he needs, he says, is a sign above the arena door, reading, 'Tonight: Olly Murs! Sold-out!' And maybe the sight of 15,000 people dancing in their seats.

—

Talking of control, Olly is recalling the first time he felt able put his foot down in the recording studio. It happened during the writing of 'Please Don't Let Me Go', one of his biggest commercial successes. During early plays, he knew the hooks were there, but some of the song's elements didn't quite seem right to him, especially in the chorus. He wanted more brass. Some of the lyrics needed reworking. After the session, Olly played the song in Mark's car and began detailing the issues bothering him.

'Maybe I'll wait and see what they come up with tomorrow,' he said.

Mark looked at him. 'Why? What you've said is totally relevant, go in there and tell 'em.'

It had never dawned on him that he could make those types of decisions before; he had lacked the confidence to mention his own creative worries at first. Making musical choices was a new thing. 'I learned from Mark that you've got to stand up. You can't just believe in something, you have to go for it.'

Olly reckons he's always been a decision maker – such as when he worked in a recruitment job, for example. 'I had the gift of the gab. I was confident, I was a fun person, I had a good energy.' He felt different operating in a recording and performing environment, though. 'When I came into this job I needed to earn my stripes,' he says. 'I think after about a year I realised that this was my career. That's when Mark said to me, "Olly you only live this once." I knew right then that I was only going to get one shot at it. Well, I might be lucky and get a second shot further down the line, but that's very unlikely.'

—

Sarah has received an email from Robbie Williams's management team. He's agreed to duet with Olly on the final night of his London residency. She reveals this development as they drive to the Barclaycard Arena for his last Birmingham show.

'Has he said what song he wants to do?' he asks.

'"Troublemaker",' she says. 'So he knows the words to that one...'

'I hope so,' says Olly. 'It's gonna be great for the fans, though. No one's gonna expect it. We'll have to piece together what we're going do. I need to have a think about it. It'll be great having Robbie down, having a laugh.'

He begins to think through how and when Robbie should arrive onstage. There is talk of bringing him up on the man-lift – the platform that launches Olly onto the front of the stage for 'Did You Miss Me' during the show's grand opening.

'You know, he's stuck to his word, Rob,' says Olly. 'He's been really kind. I'm really chuffed because I've worked with him for the last couple of years and I've always done things for him. I did his tour, which was amazing. I recorded a song with him when I did "I Wan'na Be Like You" on his *Swings Both Ways* album. It's nice that we can do something together again'.

—

There are two shows in Nottingham before the ride home to London, where he can finally enjoy the normality of home for a week – well, a homely normality comprising four sold out nights at the 02. Essex certainly delivers plenty of upsides: he can sleep in his own bed and unpack his suitcase for the first time in six weeks; Olly will drive his car to the shops and do all the menial, boring things that were almost impossible on the road. These jobs include picking up groceries in a motorway service station and making toasted crumpets for breakfast. Much of his downtime is spent in bed watching football. He later meets friends for a curry before the night concludes at his house for the early morning, heavyweight fight between Floyd Mayweather and Manny Pacquiao. 'A good Saturday night,' he says, sounding almost relieved at the mundaneness of it all.

'I live an incredible life,' he explains. 'And I could live it in an extraordinary fashion, but that would take myself away from everything that I love and everything that makes me *me*.'

He lists the trappings he might have once fallen for: a fancy house in central London maybe, or a place in one of its more salubrious suburbs. Luxurious restaurant dinners served up every night rather than home cooking. A personal driver – 'All that bollocks. But, one, it's wasteful. And, two, it's not me. I choose to try to live my life as normally as I can. Unfortunately there are times when I can't be normal because of my status, and who I am. But then I battle against that because I don't want to lose that normality, otherwise I'll become an idiot – I won't like the person that I might become. It's a conscious thing.'

Surely there must have been moments when you went on an expensive bender?

'Yeah, when I first started this job, it was crazy,' he says. 'I had my Hollywood moments. I liked to be driven into London for nights out, buying champagne here and there. My biggest extravagance has probably been my house, or a Bentley Continental GT.'

A car that costs over a hundred grand is quite a treat...

'Yeah, but it took me a couple of years to pluck up the courage to do that. I didn't want to spend that kind of money, but I thought, *You know what? You only live once.*'

Despite these extravagances, he thinks he lives for the normal. It makes him happy. 'It's what I need,' he says. 'Going out with my mates for an Indian where we all put £30 in the middle...'

—

Olly wanders around the backstage area at the O2 arena, flitting from room to room, looking bored. Though these shows are terrifyingly huge, there is an unmistakable, end-of-term vibe around the place. The corridors are eerily quiet. The behind-the-scenes buzz and noise of his previous gigs has simmered. Because much of his band live nearby, they can arrive any time before sound check, so the canteen and band dressing room is empty. Olly settles in at Sarah's makeshift office with his stylist, sorting through a variety of shoes – brogues in different colours, mainly – for his forthcoming TV appearances, which includes an appearance on *Germany's Next Top Model* and *The Paul O'Grady Show*.

Outside in the O2's bars and restaurants, there is a boozy, party spirit taking hold. It's a bank holiday weekend. Some of tonight's audience are making the most of their extra day off with an all-day binge. By the time Olly has taken the stage, his crowd are well-refreshed. They dance their way through Misirlou's cannonballing grooves; arms wave back and forth during the call-and-response chorus to 'Right Place Right Time'; when he makes his way to the second stage for 'Let Me In', a bra is hurled from the crowd. He dangles it in the air.

'You should put this back on,' he says, waving to the owner, who folds her arms self-consciously across her chest.

He double-checks the size. 'No, seriously. You should really put this back on.'

Those shows don't happen often – the nights where a crowd feels in-tune with his every step. Often it takes a song or two to bring them into the party mood. Tonight he felt as if the 02 crowd were with him from the first dance step.

'As I came out, everyone was going mental,' he says backstage. 'There wasn't a negative person in the room. There wasn't one person who I looked at who wasn't enjoying it. That was an amazing gig, and not every show is like that – it's a once in a lifetime thing. Last night was one of the best shows I've ever done.'

It's important to Olly that he savours the moments onstage, especially when things are going well. He knows his shelf life could be short. 'At some point it isn't going to be that exciting, it isn't going to be that amazing. I'm not gonna be 30 again. When I was doing my first tour at 26, I was young, dumb. I was single...'

How was it different?

'The girls loved it. As you get older, you still get that love – the women want to jump in bed with you and the guys want to have a pint with you. But at some point in my life the girls aren't gonna be saying that... It'll be a case of, "Oh you're like my uncle."'

—

Robbie Williams is one performer who can fully appreciate Olly's situation from first-hand experience. A platinum-selling artist with both Take That and as a solo phenomenon, he has grown older in public though he still commands sell-out crowds at Wembley Stadium. As promised, he shows up backstage for soundcheck on the afternoon of Olly's final London gig. He brings his manager and security guard, plus Spencer – a shaggy-haired Goldendoodle – with him. Typically, there is something of an upheaval, an expected disruption that accompanies the arrival of Britain's bestselling solo artist, and a man so famous that a tourist trail of locations attributed to his life has been unveiled in his hometown of Stoke-on-Trent.

The backstage area is cleared of anyone not required for soundcheck, while a strict no-photos policy is enforced by Tony. This is par for the course.

When Robbie arrives, dressed in skinny black jeans, grey T-shirt and black jacket (his hair is shaved at the sides; a swept back fringe has been bleached white) the scene is reminiscent of two reunited team-mates. There are hugs. Robbie steps back, looking Olly up and down. 'Bloody hell,' he laughs, 'looking good mate. What have you been doing?'

Olly talks through his backstage training sessions, 'Mate, it's hardcore. But, hang on, you're in great shape, too...'

'Cheers Oll,' he says. 'No, I am, but I don't want to look like a doorman. I don't want to look like I'm guarding the door at Yates's Wine Lodge. The label in my clothes hasn't said "M" for a long time. Seriously, it's been six, seven days since I came off tour and I am knackered. Maybe my hormones are imbalanced, but I'm proper knackered.'

He says he'd quite like some props to distract the audience from his onstage fatigue. 'The older I get, the more stuff I want around me so I can go, "Look at these guys!" Or, "Look at this mechanical whale!"'

Robbie has more questions, so they head into a spare dressing room for some catch-up time, away from their respective management teams. Only Spencer joins them for the chat.

'So, I'm walking in with Spencer,' says Robbie. 'I'm at the back of the arena, for *your* show, and it struck me: this is the bloody O2! Then I began wondering about where you came from, and where you are now. Mate, do you still pinch yourself? Because I stopped pinching myself a while ago...'

Olly laughs, disbelievingly. 'Come on,' he says. 'You did Knebworth, stadiums with Take That, stadiums on your own. Knebworth was huge.'

'But you were working in a call centre...'

Olly laughs. 'Yeah, 100% it's amazing to do the O2. But at the same time, the last tour I did was yours. I remember the first show was in Ireland. When I came out, it hit me just how many people there were.'

Robbie nods, almost sagely.

'Ah, yes. You can't just *un-see* stadiums.'

—

'Look at Ed Sheeran,' says Olly. 'Wouldn't you just love to be backstage and go, "You know what? I'm gonna do a gig in front of 80,000 people, just me and my guitar. I haven't got a band, I haven't got to pay anyone..."' Olly says laughing.

Robbie agrees, though he recognises the limitations to their individual stagecraft. 'But we can't play anything,' he says. 'We're not real. We didn't learn how to do that.'

He begins dancing on the spot. 'We only learned how to go, "*Hiya!* Hands in the air!" You can play the guitar a bit though...'

'Yeah, and we've got a bit in the show where there's a piano and we play three of my old songs.'

The words hang in the air briefly. Robbie seems to be counting the years since Olly's career began in 2009. 'You've got... *old songs*?'

—

'To be honest,' says Robbie, now standing onstage, 'I only know a verse.'

They're pacing along the catwalk that extends into the O2's vast dance floor, working out where best to stand for their duet on 'Troublemaker'. It's been agreed that Robbie should arrive at the front of the stage, jumping up on the man-lift for dramatic effect. As the band run through the funky intro, Robbie scans a printed copy of the lyrics. "It's like you're always there in the corners of my mind," he sings slowly. "I see your silhouette every time I close my eyes. There must be poison in those fingertips of yours, cos I keep coming back for more..."

Olly looks pleased. 'There's going to be such a massive reaction,' he says. 'The crowd are gonna go nuts.'

Olly manoeuvres Robbie to a second man-lift positioned at the back of the stage. From there, it's suggested they descend together, slowly, as the song closes out.

'It's a bit snug though,' says Olly, as the pair of them stand close together. The lift begins to drop.

'Don't be shy, mate,' says Robbie. 'I've seen you in the showers at Soccer Aid. Come on, let's go bulge to bulge...'

—

After the soundcheck, they move into Olly's dressing room, where Francesca, his mum, Vicky, and his grandparents, Nana and Pops, are waiting. They poke fun at Pop's Access All Areas pass – apparently, on first receiving one, he believed the triple As stamped across the laminate card stood for 'Anytime. Anyplace. Anywhere.'

'Thing is,' says Robbie, looking sheepish, 'it was only when you told me that story that I clued into what Triple A actually meant. I had no idea. I get it now...'

He slaps Olly on the thigh. 'So, congratulations, mate!'

'Thanks mate,' says Olly, though he looks confused. 'For what?'

'For the gig,' says Robbie. 'Right?'

'What gig? Oh, *X Factor*! Are you doing it, too?' He's heard whispers that Robbie might be joining Simon Cowell's revamped judging line-up. 'Come on...'

Robbie shakes his head. He says he'd rather take a presenting role than a position on the panel. Olly's eyes suddenly light up. 'We'd be like Morecambe and Wise!' he says.

'More like Little and Large,' says Robbie. 'We should do something together at some point, though.'

Olly nods. He then announces he was struck by an idea along the same lines, not long ago. 'But I don't want you to nick it,' he says.

Robbie raises a hand, a mock 'scout's honour' gesture. 'I swear.'

'OK, well, I wanna do a swing album. Obviously you and Michael Bublé have done them successfully...'

Vicky butts in. 'And Rod Stewart.'

'Yeah, and Rod Stewart. But I was thinking of doing a two-disc album where I did some old songs, but on the second album I want to cover top hits from the last 20 years – Rihanna, Bruno Mars. I'd cover one of yours...

'Anyway, what I was thinking was that me, you, maybe Gary Barlow, Bublé, we could do a Rat Pack-style show at the Royal Albert Hall. We'll do our own songs, covers, duets, it could be a really fun night.'

Robbie laughs. He suddenly breaks into a jazzy version of 'She's The One'. 'I was her... She was me... And if there's somebody... Calling me on...' He clicks his fingers and winks. 'She's the one.'

—

To Olly, Rob is a proper mate, but he understands the unreliable currency of friendships within his line of work. It's why he surrounds himself with people he can trust, like Sarah and Mark.

'I love being around normal, fun, down to earth people,' he says, now alone backstage. 'Honesty is important. I feel that this industry is swallowed up by a lot of self-centred, arrogant, crap people that tell you what you want to hear. They tell you how amazing you are. They live off your name and try to be your best mate. They're people you talk to, but they're not mates. They're not real people. They try to live a fake life.'

—

'I might not have the best voice in the world,' he'll say later. 'But it's a talent to go out on your own and do a live show. Me, and Rob, and Michael Bublé: the reason we make it easy is because we go out there and talk. It's a bit of banter, and it's natural. It takes a natural talent to do that – it's hard to do it, but it's easy for me. I love going out there. I love performing. I can't think of anything better in my life, and my world, than to go out there on that stage in front of 15,000 people. It feels natural. I don't have any nerves, I just go out there and enjoy it.'

—

Later that night, at the close of the show, Robbie emerges from the stage to a rush of screams. Mobile phone cameras flash. Despite the concerns, his lyrics are nailed, Olly joining him at the front of the catwalk as they link arms for the chorus: 'I say, "I'm done!" but then you pull me back, I swear you're giving me a heart attack... Troublemaker!'

Later, the pair of them descend, 'bulge-to-bulge', as the house lights blitz different colours above them. The yelling and cheering threatens to drown out even Dexter's heavy drum attack. Confetti guns fire. When Robbie gets to the back of the stage, Spencer is waiting to join him for the car ride home. Onstage, 'Troublemaker' is still playing out, but Robbie and his shaggy-haired companion are already out of the door, job done.

—

It's been a successful night. In one shift, Olly has finished the last of four nights at the 02, performed a duet with his mate Robbie Williams, and filmed what will later become a live DVD release – throughout the show, cameras trailed his every move onstage. There was only one glitch, however. As he danced across the catwalk during 'Wrapped Up', his foot slipped on a towel lying in the darkness. The tumble caused him to hit the floor with a painful bump. Despite all his achievements tonight, it's the one thing that will bug him as he drives all the way home to Essex, presumably for more crumpets.

OLLY ON THE RECORD: MAKING MUSIC

It's funny, I can't listen to other musicians when I'm on tour. Yeah, I'll put something on when I'm in my dressing room, to get me pumped up for the show. I'll listen to anything. I'll throw on whatever I feel like from R&B, to some heavy metal – anything that comes to mind.

I don't always do that, though. It only happens when I need a bit of a buzz, or a kick. But to be honest with you, I don't really need that much of an extra buzz or a kick when I'm about to play the O2. And when I go home after a show, I switch off. Music isn't a part of my life at that moment.

I guess I listen to a lot more music when I'm writing an album. That's when I want to get an influence, some new ideas. It's good to get inspiration from other singers that I love and admire. But when I've finished an album, and I'm singing all the time, or I'm out every day performing, I don't want to listen to anyone else. I don't need to be inspired. Because I'm performing I'm just focused on the job at hand – my own songs and lyrics.

I've never been the kind of artist who's constantly thinking about writing new material, or coming up with ideas for fresh lyrics or songs. On this tour it was the first opportunity I'd had to play the songs from *Never Been Better*, so I focused solely on that.

Chapter Eleven

NO BETTER FEELING

NO BETTER FEELING

'Tonight it's gonna kick *off*!' shouts Olly. He's sitting in the back of the people carrier driving him north along the M1. Yesterday was a busy day. He finished filming what should have been a fairly routine promo video for his next single, 'Beautiful to Me' – 'Just a cameo appearance really, but it took ages.' This was followed with several radio interviews. Work was completed with a stripped-back show in the Covent Garden member's venue, The Hospital Club – a private gig for competition winners and corporate sponsors.

Tomorrow promises to be just as busy. He begins filming on *X Factor* in Manchester where he'll be joined by co-presenter Caroline Flack, plus a crowd of auditioning hopefuls, at an outdoor stage. Olly seems unfazed by the workload, however. He announces that, tonight, after his final show on the *Never Been Better* tour in Liverpool, he plans on getting drunk with his band, the crew, some close mates and Francesca in Playground, a city centre club. A hangover is likely to accompany his TV debut as Simon Cowell's latest frontman.

'It's gonna be no-holds-barred tonight,' he says. 'I'm going for it. They'll be getting a naughty Olly Murs onstage.' He starts shouting again. 'Liverpool! You are *getting it*!'

Apart from nights in Cardiff and Manchester, Olly's partying has been low-key so far. He leans forward to where Mark is sitting in the front and grabs his shoulders. 'It's Saturday night, Marky-boy! If you're not with me at half past three when I'm walking out of that club tomorrow morning…' Mark is nearly ten years Olly's senior and married with two kids. He seems less than thrilled with Olly's off-the-leash attitude. 'Now, Oll, you know that isn't going to be the case…'

Olly continues with the threat. '... there's gonna be some ructions.'

Despite this bolshiness, Olly's mood is mixed today. He says he's looking forward to unwinding at his end-of-tour party, but he'd rather the trip wasn't ending at all. Pretty much every night so far has been fun and he thinks coming off the road will bring him down a little. 'Gutted,' is the word he uses when asked to describe the closing of his UK run. 'Really gutted,' he repeats. 'It's been a great laugh. I'm not relieved that it's over at all. I'm going to be a bit sad tomorrow. I love touring, though there are always stresses and worries...'

Like what?

'I mean, the biggest one has always been making sure that I'm in shape and fit every night; that my voice is in good nick for the show. There's only been a couple of gigs where I haven't felt that confident going onstage, but when the songs have started and the set kicks in, it all comes together.'

Mark turns around. 'Bit different now though, Oll, eh?' he says. 'Remember those early shows? When you first started?'

Olly smiles. Then he winces. He can recall the first 12 months of performing, making appearances in over-18 clubs as part of an *X Factor* tour, and it wasn't glamorous work. He often found himself playing to audiences of around 700 people – 'I'd be doing a few covers, like Robbie's "She's The One" and the Beatles' "Twist and Shout". There was "Can You Feel It" by the Jackson Five, a Tina Turner song, and Queen's "Don't Stop Me Now".' The workload was big. He estimates there were over 100 shows in his debut year. Mark, by then installed as his official tour manager, provided support.

'I was security, driver, sound engineer, tour manager, king of the world,' says Mark. 'I *dominated*. The club circuit didn't know what'd hit it.'

Back then, Olly's stage set-up was comparatively modest. There were no multistorey platforms, scissor lifts or descending walkways. 'It was just me and a backing track, no band,' he says. 'We did sweaty, horrible clubs. People forget that. They think I just came off *X Factor*, released a single, went to number one and then everything worked out from there. Happy days. But it wasn't like that. I toured for a year, doing little club circuits and corporate gigs. I remember playing a racecourse, the one in York, as part of an *X Factor* thing. There were 35,000 people in the crowd and it was insane. I was bricking it beforehand. I didn't have any of my own songs, but we still smashed it with the covers.'

Did it ever seem overwhelming?

'No, I never thought it was too much. *X Factor* was so popular at the time, and so big, that everyone wanted us. It stepped up once I'd released 'Please Don't Let Me Go', my own single, though. That became a hit really quickly – we beat Katy Perry to number one. Everything took off after that.'

Mark turns around. 'But to be fair to you, you soaked it all up like a sponge,' he says, proudly. 'At that point you didn't know what was ahead of you. You took it all in and it got better, and better, and better. You were born to do it, mate – I don't care what anyone says, you're a born pop star.'

—

Olly hates the term 'pop star'. It irritates him. When people ask him what he does for a living, maybe at the immigration desk in an American airport, he'll explain that he's a singer, or an entertainer. Despite his line of work, and the celebrities he mixes with, he doesn't like it when people refer to themselves as being 'stars'.

'Like when someone gets signed by a record company and then they go, "Oh, I'm a pop star now..." I think that's really pretentious.'

So how do you describe yourself?

'I just say, "entertainer" because, I dunno, I do a bit of everything. If I was going over to do some filming in America, I'd say I was an entertainer, or a TV presenter. I wouldn't say that I was a singer, even though to a lot of people I am. That's just me, though. I think if I was to go through passport control and say "I'm a singer" or "pop star" they're just gonna think, "Oh yeah? Here we go..."'

—

As the people carrier makes its way through Liverpool, Olly talks through his forthcoming schedule. More TV appearances have been planned beyond the tour, plus a trip to Europe for several shows – Germany, Italy, Sweden, among others – though they'll be smaller than the arenas he's been playing recently. Less thrilling are the weeks at home where he'll have nothing to focus on. Sitting around on the sofa, watching TV bores him.

'I've never, ever been a couch potato,' he says. 'There might be a couple of days where I'll lie in front of the TV, but I couldn't imagine living like that when I retire. Doing nothing for the rest of my life? No thanks.'

Olly suddenly predicts the end of his career. 'I'll probably die onstage,' he says, dramatically. 'Yeah, I probably will.'

He goes quiet for a moment.

'Well, I say that I'd like to die onstage, though I don't think the people around me or my family would like to see that. But seriously, I'd rather die doing something that I loved.'

Chatting to Robbie at the 02 has got him thinking about longevity. As the younger of the two, Olly has yet to encounter the insecurities that arrive with advancing years – changing looks, the extra wrinkles and curves that appear at middle age – though he understands that pop careers can sometimes hinge on appearances as well as hooky hits. He reckons that for as long as he has the energy to perform, he'll be OK.

'I think I've got a very different mindset to Robbie in many ways,' he says. 'That might change when I get to 40. We've all taken a couple of days to get over shows, but I'm still in good shape. I look at people like Ryan Giggs and other sportsmen who have competed well into their forties. They've proved that it's achievable. I can keep myself in good condition if I eat the right foods, train well and do some yoga. That stuff can re-energise you.'

The fact that he loves his job helps too, he says. There have been times on this tour when he's felt tired. Some mornings have been trickier than others, but the shows tend to incentivise him. 'There's no better feeling than getting out there and performing onstage. For me, I just get out there and do it. But who knows? I might be like Robbie in ten years' time. I'll be talking to a young whippersnapper like me, asking him, "How do you do it…"'

—

Olly falls asleep on the backseat. As his breathing deepens, Mark craftily snaps a picture. He starts to whisper conspiratorially. 'Right, here's the deal with tonight,' he says. 'At the end of every tour, we always play a few pranks on Oll. It's become a bit of a tradition over the years.'

He recalls how, one time, when Olly was lowered on a scissor lift, he was greeted with the sight of his road crew sitting around a poker table beneath the stage, playing cards. On other occasions, band members have worn novelty wigs and swapped instruments. It's been fairly low-key stuff. 'But we're going to up the stakes a bit this time.'

Moments later, a photograph of Olly, snoring lightly, is posted to 6.4 million followers on his official Twitter account.

—

Everyone is in on tonight's pranks, except Olly.

As he settles into his dressing room backstage for a session of FIFA time, Mark gathers the band together for a meeting. There are a couple of hours to go before the show starts, and he wants to ensure that everyone's prepared for

what should be a chaotic finale. This is not a free-for-all, he warns; he stresses the word 'professionalism'.

'Right everyone, it's the last night of the tour,' he says. 'So this is where the fun and games begin. Here's what I'm thinking: basically it's Olly's birthday next week and we've got him a cake. My idea is to put it on the piano and when it comes up for "Seasons", I'll be sat at it, pretending to play "Happy Birthday" – though Sean, you'll have to play the actual song from your keyboard.'

Sean nods. 'That'll work. Just don't touch the keys...'

'No, I'm not, I'm just gonna say, "OK, Olly, hang on... As you may or may not know everyone, it's Olly's birthday next week." And I'll get everyone to sing.'

Mark then explains that there will be plenty of action going on behind the scenes.

'This won't affect any of you, but when he comes down for the costume change before "Heart Skips a Beat", there won't be anyone in the dressing area, apart from me and Tony. We'll have some boxing gloves on, having a sparring match. That'll freak him out. But don't worry, I'll get him onstage in time for the song.'

He's saving the best prank until last, however. 'I've spoken to the comedian John Bishop – he's here. Remember the Robbie situation, when he popped up for the second verse of "Troublemaker"? Well, John's going to pop up tonight. He won't know the words, so it'll be a complete mickey-take and Olly won't know what's going on. They'll just sing it out, the two of them, and go off together on the man-lift.'

Sean is concerned about John's connection to the rest of the band. Though he's an experienced TV entertainer, and an arena headliner in his own right, the stage set-up might seem unfamiliar. Plus, he won't have the same in-ear monitors, as worn by Olly. Hearing anything over the noise of the crowd could prove impossible, but Mark doesn't seem too bothered.

'Yeah, well that just adds to it,' he says.

Later, there's talk of the road crew and how to involve them. Somebody suggests swapping the band with stage hands during a moment of crowd interaction; Olly always introduces the audience to his supporting musicians at a fixed point in the show.

'Great!' laughs Mark.

Someone else mentions a tweak. 'Can we get the big roadies, though, not the nice-looking ones...?'

—

Onstage, Olly is leading the crowd through 'Why Do I Love You', but in a guest box above the dance floor, John Bishop is experiencing stage fright. He sends a text explaining his unease, so Mark runs to the VIP area to cajole him.

'Listen, John, it's going to be fine,' he says, dragging him away from his seat.

'I just don't wanna be standing there like an idiot,' says John, looking remarkably reticent for a man overly familiar with cracking jokes in front of an arena-sized audience.

Mark reassures him. 'No, no, it's gonna be fine. Look, we did it the other night.

The element of surprise is what makes it funny. The spotlight will be on you. Olly will be behind and everyone will be going, "Who the hell is that?!" Then they'll get it. You'll only have to sing a little bit of the song. In fact, I don't care if you sing "Ba Ba Black Sheep", it'll be fine. It'll be funny, everyone's gonna laugh.'

John starts singing, 'Why does it feel so good but hurt so bad...' What he lacks in harmony, he more than makes up for in effort. Mark gees him along. 'My mind keeps saying, "Run as fast as you can". I say, "I'm done", but then you pull me back...'

Mark has delivered a convincing appeal. 'Beautiful! You don't even have to do that much...'

John looks a little offended. 'Look, if I'm gonna be on there, *I'm gonna be on there*.'

—

With a birthday cake delivered, and a switcheroo with his band and road crew completed to typically confusing results, Olly readies himself for 'Troublemaker'. Unbeknown to him, behind the stage in the costume changeover tent, John Bishop is squeezing himself into a two-sizes-too-small top – a pink T-shirt. One of Olly's lyrics, 'YOU'VE GOT ME WRAPPED UP' is emblazoned across the front. He looks edgy – 'I'm terrified,' he says.

Surely you're used to performing to crowds of this size though?

'Yeah, but I've never had to bloody sing before.'

He chooses this moment to drop to the floor for a series of push-ups. 'Just pumping myself up,' he says.

Mark pokes his head inside. It's time. 'Ready mate?'

John sucks in a deep, settling breath. 'As ready as I'm gonna be.' Moments later, he springs onstage, mic in hand. At first Olly doesn't spot him. His back is turned; the loud cheers, he thinks, are for him. It's only when an unusual, slightly out-of tune-voice booms over his own, that he turns to see the comedian dancing at the front of the stage.

'Hah! John Bishop everyone!' he yells, barely missing a beat and dancing towards him. He pulls him close and guides him around the stage. Olly even leads the crowd in a singalong.

'Bishop! Bishop! Bishop!' he yells.

'Oi! Oi! Oi!' they respond, before the pair of them disappear from view on the man-lift. They hug at the back of the stage.

'John that was bloody brilliant!' laughs Olly, now readying himself for an encore. 'I didn't expect that at all. I didn't even know you were there at first, I thought, *Who's this person singing in my ear?* And there's you, with one of my T-shirts on, in pink, and it's really tight fitting, too. Ridiculous!'

John doesn't seem too enamoured with the highs of being a singer in front of a huge crowd. 'I couldn't hear a bloody thing,' he moans.

—

Olly's end-of-tour party begins backstage. Several mates from Essex, including Mace, have travelled up to join him, as has Francesca. John Bishop joins a guest list sprinkled with football celebrity – Everton manager, Roberto Martinez arrives with his coaching staff and their wives; former Liverpool captain and *Soccer Saturday* pundit, Phil Thompson has flown from his Sky TV commitments in Middlesex to be here. Another pundit, the recently retired England international Jamie Carragher will also join the party when it moves to a private room in Playground, where the gathering will rack up a bar bill in the tens of thousands. The last anyone sees of Olly, he is guzzling from a very large bottle of Dom Pérignon.

—

In the people carrier, hungover and tired the next morning, Olly is travelling to his first *X Factor* filming session, which is due to take place at EventCity in Manchester. Dressed in grey blazer, white T-shirt and skinny-fit black jeans, the plan is for him to present a couple of short links in front of a live audience – several hundred people waiting to audition before a panel of production-team judges. Their hope is to make it through this preliminary round. Success will give them the chance to perform before the show's more recognisable tastemakers, which includes perennial panto-villain figure, Simon Cowell – Olly's boss.

Olly's hope, meanwhile, is to make it through the day without looking hungover. He recounts last night's drinking tally – there was champagne, he remembers. Beer, vodka, a singalong of old school garage hits on the tour bus. Were there shots? He's not sure – probably. He thinks he might have managed two hours' sleep in total. 'I'll be alright,' he shrugs.

Sarah, who joins him today, along with Mark and Mellissa, points out that part of the filming requires him to drive an *X Factor*-branded van towards the outdoor stage. Apparently, the route will be lined by screaming fans.

This is very different to his first ever filmed *X Factor* episode – the one in 2009, which saw him progress into the live stages of the show. To appreciate the scale of his changing fortunes over the years, it's worth listening to his recollections of this surreal moment.

'It was just an out-of-body experience,' he says. 'I remember being backstage waiting to go on, and hearing people getting told "NO" by the judges.'

He remembers his walk along to the audition room, a production-team member standing alongside him. Presenter, Dermot O'Leary – the man he will, in an around hour, replace as the show's studio focal point – came into view. He wished Olly good luck. Somebody, a member of the TV crew, or a runner, he's not sure, readied his microphone before flashing the thumbs-up sign, Olly's cue to face the panel.

'Then the audience went quiet,' he says. 'I walked out, they cheered, but I didn't even look at the judges, I was trying to find the "X". The crew had told me to walk onto one that was marked on the floor. That's when I looked up and saw four famous faces. I'd never seen anyone famous before...'

No one?

'No one! And there was Louis Walsh, Danni Minogue, Cheryl Cole and bloody Simon Cowell.'

He sounds incredulous. 'Simon Cowell was talking to *me*! But when I opened my mouth to talk back, I spoke like an absolute fish. I had no form of conversation. I couldn't even remember my name, or how old I was, or where I lived. It was a rush. I could see so many people. I thought, *Is this actually happening*?'

He delivered a two-and-a-half-minute version of Stevie Wonder's single, 'Superstition'. His singing drew appreciative nods from the judges. 'It was a blur,' says Olly. But he knew his audition had been impressive, the cheers from the crowd told him that at least. Simon Cowell then confirmed his successful showing. 'I've got to tell you, Olly,' he said. 'This is the easiest "yes" I've ever given.'

In the people carrier, Olly shakes his head. Six years on he still struggles to comprehend the lightning bolt moment. 'I thought, *Oh my god is this really happening?* In my head I wanted to say, "Are you guys really sure you wanna say yes to me? What the hell?" Then all I could think was, *I've got through! That wasn't supposed to happen.* It was crazy, a crazy experience. But every night was an amazing experience on *X Factor*. Something I'll never forget.'

—

Today could represent an auspicious moment in Olly's career. He marks the opening minutes of his new job by telling Caroline Flack about his drinking session the previous evening. 'We got messy,' he says as they meet in a dressing room at EventCity. '*Battered*.'

She eyes him up and down and pokes fun at his trim figure. 'So, what time did you go to bed then?' she asks, prodding him in the stomach. 'I bet it was only two o'clock...'

'Half four,' says Olly proudly.

X Factor's executive producer, Amelia Brown, begins readying them both with scripts. There are details on camera positions and instructions for where they'll be standing during the filmed introductions.

'That's what I like to hear, Olly,' Amelia says, sarcastically. 'It's day one and you're already sounding professional: "Yeah, I'm gonna nail this one for you guys."'

Olly laughs. 'Look, I'd run a marathon for you today if I had to... I'd finish last, though.'

—

Despite his hangover, Olly seems remarkably focused on his new role – both on and off camera. 'We need to catch up,' he says to Amelia. 'I want to make sure everything's spot on.' There's a headline he spotted in today's edition of the *Sun*. Apparently long-term judge Louis Walsh is leaving the show. 'Is that right?'

One of the team nods.

'*Wow.*' Then he recalls the leak regarding his own appointment. 'I spoke to Simon in his house and the next day it was in the paper: "Olly's coming on *X Factor*!"'

He starts looking through the script cards. 'I'm excited to be a presenter though,' he says. 'I couldn't be horrible to people, like the panellists. I'm a man of the people.'

Amelia flashes him a quizzical look. 'Sorry, did you just say, "I'm a man of the people?"'

'Yeah... haha. No wait, I'm the people's champion!'

This is a jokey reference Olly sometimes uses when regarding his second-placed position in the 2009 final. He sees his subsequent chart success as confirmation of a popularity beyond the show. 'I first mentioned "the people's champion" thing one night on *Xtra Factor*,' he continues. 'And Caroline also went, "Did you really just say that?" I was like, "Yeah, but that's what the *people* said." For two years, she's slaughtered me over it...'

He scans his script, and plays out his opening moments on the studio floor. 'Welcome to *X Factor*!' he announces to the room. 'It's Saturday night, yeah! Welcome to the show, here are the 12 contestants... We'll be hoping for your votes. Make sure you pick up the phones and get voting tonight because it's gonna be an exciting show, isn't it, Caroline?'

Olly points to an empty space where his co-presenter will, at some point in the future, be standing. 'She'll waffle on... *Bosh!* Then I'll come back. "OK, so first up I'm going to introduce you to the judges – forces of nature all of them... The judges everyone! Simon Cowell!"'

He makes a grand, sweeping gesture with his arm. Presenting *X Factor* looks like the easiest thing in the world all of a sudden.

—

For a hangover of this magnitude there is always junk food. An emergency package arrives comprising McDonald's breakfasts. Olly grabs a muffin. Egg and cheese oozes through the wrapper.

'Here, Caroline, do you like my hair?' he says, taking a bite from the droopy sandwich.

'Nah.'

'Bitch!' he laughs. 'I've changed it... Oi! What do you care anyway, Miss Coming Fifth in *FHM*'s Sexiest Woman of the Year Competition? You're up there with all the supermodels!'

Caroline adopts a mock-diva tone. 'Well, yeah, it was to be expected after my time on *Strictly Come Dancing* – joking.'

Olly looks a bit miffed. 'Eighty-three. I was number 83 in the world's fittest male – that's crap.'

She laughs at Olly's wounded pride.

'And I was fifth? Looks like I'm the people's champion when it comes to the world's sexiest...'

—

Olly, stands alongside Caroline, looks into the camera and prepares to deliver the first lines of his second *X Factor* career. With hair and make-up completed, he looks remarkably healthy for a man with only a few hours' sleep to his name.

'Welcome to *X Factor*!' he says as a suspended camera swoops down towards him. 'Thousands of people have applied to change their lives forever, but who is next?'

'It could be you!' says Caroline pointing to a girl in the crowd. She gestures to another. 'It could be you.'

Olly looks into the camera. 'It could be *you*.'

The crowds squeezed around his stage start to scream and cheer. Cannons fire jets of flame behind him. For this multi-platinum-selling artist, latest face of Saturday night telly, and eighty-third sexiest man in the world, the completion of a 28-night arena tour has been marked with another beginning, a new chapter. The entertainer from *X Factor* has come full circle.

OLLY ON THE RECORD: MY FUTURE

I don't like looking too far ahead in my life. I just like to live for what's now, in the moment – day-by-day, week-by-week. In my head, I know I've got loads to do this year and next, but I'm not thinking about that. There's going to be some exciting things for my fans to get stuck into, like *X Factor*, a DVD, there's even talk of doing a documentary on my life. Beyond that there will be some new songs and I'll be back in the studio for my next album.

I don't like to wish my life away, though. On tour, I tried not to look too far ahead. I would say to myself, 'OK, so there's a show tonight. Tomorrow I'm gonna rest up in bed, or play some golf with friends.' I didn't want to look beyond the next 24 hours or so. I wanted to keep my focus on what was coming up immediately. If I'd started thinking about *X Factor* or my next album while I was on the road, it would have changed my focus. Instead, I rode the wave, and dealt with things as and when they came up.

I also believe that if you think about a future project too much, you can over-analyse it and balls it up. Picking the bones out of what might or might not happen in the future has never helped me. Like the *X Factor* job. I had time to mull the decision over when I was on tour. I made up my mind, decided that I wanted to do it, and signed the contract. Beyond that, I didn't think about what was going to happen. I just rocked up on the first day of work, and thought, *Right, let's do it!* And it was such an exciting day.

That's not to say there aren't things that I've fantasised about doing later in life. I'd love to travel again – on my own. And I'd want to see parts of the world that I haven't been to yet. It would be great to do that on a good budget, so I could experience it in some style. I remember when I went backpacking around Australia in 2008, I ended up in some hostels that were pretty scary. I won't be doing that again!

At the moment there's no rush to book that kind of thing, but it's something I wanna do. All I know is that I'm massively excited about everything coming up. And I can't wait to get into the next adventure...

ENCORE

It was the party I never wanted to end.

Twenty-eight gigs, hundreds of thousands of tickets sold, a ton of hit singles and album favourites being played to arenas packed with amazing fans: the *Never Been Better* tour 2015 was as good is gets – well, so far anyway. But believe me, walking offstage on that final night in Liverpool was a weird sensation. Yeah, I was still buzzing from the experience of performing in front of all those people, but a little part of me felt sad. As far as I'm concerned, there's no better feeling than being onstage. It's what I live for. When it gets taken away from me, even for a short period of time – like at the end of a tour, say – it leaves a pretty big void.

For some artists, filling four nights at the 02 in London, or three nights in Manchester, as well as playing arena shows up and down the country, would be enough. Not me. I want more, and the longer I go on as a performer, the bigger I want to get. I once had a taste of playing the super-big shows, to crowds of 60,000, even 70,000 people, and I want another piece of that.

In my head, the next challenge for me is to get big enough to play a stadium, just like Ed Sheeran, One Direction and Coldplay in the past. A big ask? Maybe, but I'm going to give it a damn good go, though I know a lot of work still needs to be done.

To get there, I reckon I'm going to need another number one album, maybe two, and some massive hit singles. I feel like I'm making progress, though. Next year I'm going back into the studio to make my fifth album. A sixth will follow a year later, and I quite fancy doing a swing album with some modern covers, a bit like Mark Ronson did with his 2007 album, *Version*. But whatever happens I'm not going to hold back, and with all my amazing fans behind me, I know that just about anything's possible.

It's not just in the studio where there's some work to be done. My touring has also got bigger every year. When I first stepped out on the road in 2010, my expectations were low. I figured, 'If I can get to a second album then I'm gonna be laughing.' By March 2015, the bar had been raised, big time, and I wanted to live up to the name on ticket. I wanted to prove to people that, as an artist, as an entertainer, I'd *never been better*. I've felt on top of my game for some time now. Hopefully my UK tour hammered home that idea to a lot of other people.

It's fired me up, too. If I've learned one thing from this tour it's that I should appreciate every second onstage because, believe me, there's no better feeling than seeing 15,000 fans in Dublin, or Sheffield, singing the lyrics of my songs back at me. It's a huge rush. If I could bottle that buzz, I'd be drinking it every day. That's why I know how hard it would be to walk away from a life like this. A lot of artists have left the business only to struggle. They missed the highs of performing and got into boozing, drugs, even gambling, to make up for the excitement of performing. I won't ever jump into that lifestyle, I'm not that type of character, but it makes me very aware of the fact that I have to live in the moment, and enjoy the now.

But even that's not enough for me. I want to improve as a singer, a performer and a showman. And that's where *X Factor* comes in. Over the coming year I'm going to learn whether I've got it as TV presenter, which is a massively exciting challenge – I'm hoping that me and Caroline can go onto one of the biggest shows on the telly and smash it together. It might also open a whole new life for me. Yeah, I love the music. I love touring, and I love doing everything I'm involved in right now. But do I see myself performing in front of arenas for the next 30 years? I'm not so sure.

Maybe I'll still be going if I'm a household name. Otherwise, I'll be happy working in TV, or making the most of some other opportunity that might come my way. See that's the thing with me – I'll never say, 'never' to anything. If somebody asks me to do something that's a little bit leftfield, like I don't know, acting maybe, then why not? If an idea excites me, I'll go for it, but only if it seems inspiring. If not, I won't take it, no matter how much cash they're offering.

All I know is that I'm not going to fade away. I'm going out with a bang. It might be onstage at Wembley Stadium in front of 70,000 people, or it might be on TV. Either way it's going to be bloody exciting. So far, my career has been an insane journey. From an *X Factor* hopeful in 2009 to *X Factor* presenter in 2015, with a sold-out arena tour of the UK under my belt: there's been no half-measures as of yet. And there's no point in letting up now.

Stay cheeky.

#NEVERBEENBETTERTOUR

First published in Great Britain in 2015 by Coronet
An imprint of Hodder & Stoughton
An Hachette UK company

1

A CIP catalogue record for this title is available from the British Library
ISBN 9781473618107
Printed in Germany by Mohnmedia Mohndruck GmbH, Gütersloh

Hodder & Stoughton policy is to use papers that are natural, renewable and
recyclable products and made from wood grown in sustainable forests.
The logging and manufacturing processes are expected to conform to the
environmental regulations of the country of origin.

Hodder & Stoughton Ltd
Carmelite House
50 Victoria Embankment
London EC4Y 0DZ
www.hodder.co.uk